TURNAROUND TIME:

The Best
of Computerworld's
Q and A's

Larry Long

Prentice Hall
Englewood Cliffs, New Jersey 07632

Library of Congress Cataloging-in-Publication Data

Long, Larry E. (date)
  Turnaround time.

    Includes index.
  1. Electronic data processing—Management.
  2. Electronic data processing—Miscellanea. I. Title.
QA76.9.M3L66 1988   004′.068   87–13934
ISBN 0-13-933029-1

Editorial/production supervision
  and interior design: *Gloria L. Jordan*
Cover design: *Lundgren Graphics, Ltd.*
Manufacturing buyer: *S. Gordon Osbourne*

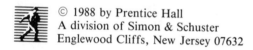
Computerworld is the registered trademark of IDG
Communications, Framingham, MA 01701

Printed in the United States of America
10 9 8 7 6 5 4 3 2 1

ISBN 0-13-933029-1 025

Prentice-Hall International (UK) Limited, *London*
Prentice-Hall of Australia Pty. Limited, *Sydney*
Prentice-Hall Canada Inc., *Toronto*
Prentice-Hall Hispanoamericana, S.A., *Mexico*
Prentice-Hall of India Private Limited, *New Delhi*
Prentice-Hall of Japan, Inc., *Tokyo*
Simon & Schuster Asia Pte. Ltd., *Singapore*
Editora Prentice-Hall do Brasil, Ltda., *Rio de Janeiro*

Contents

Preface

BACKGROUND

My "Turnaround Time" column first appeared in the February 18, 1980 edition of *Computerworld*. That first column contained: *questions* and *answers* (Q&A's) concerning an MIS progress report to an executive committee, the most pressing issue in data processing, interviewing strategies, system documentation, and user training in a hostile environment. These questions are representative of the focus of "Turnaround Time" during its six-year run—the people-side of computers and MIS. This book is a categorized compilation of the best of "Turnaround Time" Q&A's.

I must admit that I wrote only half of this book. Your colleagues, friends, and others in the computer community wrote the other half—anonymously, of course. Together, we have examined the world of computers from a good many perspectives. Thousands of people have made inquiries to me and through "Turnaround Time," I have *responded* to hundreds of questions from analysts, company presidents, students, professors, MIS management in every area, user management in every major area, veteran and entry-level programmers, vendors of hardware and software, unemployed computer specialists, education coordinators, MIS auditors, spouses of programmers, lawyers, physicians, entrepreneurs, consultants, entire project teams, government officials, and many more. I have also responded to representatives from scores of societies and special-interest groups.

The majority of the "Turnaround Time" Q&A's that appear here are timeless and as applicable today as when they first appeared in *Computerworld*. Others have been updated to reflect today's circumstances.

AUDIENCE

Most computer/MIS books deal with specific topics: hardware, software, methods, procedures, and so on. This book is unique in that it deals with a plethora of everyday problems, concerns, and situations that can be found in any organization. It is a reference book for computer/MIS specialists, MIS managers, user managers, and top management. It is a casebook for MIS and business professors and students. It also provides interesting and informative reading material for anyone directly or indirectly associated with the computer community.

CONTENT AND ORGANIZATION

The Q&A's that have appeared in "Turnaround Time" reflect real people and real circumstances. Although my response is to a particular question, in most instances, both the "Q" and "A" are applicable to many people and a variety of organizations. Indeed, one of the primary criteria for inclusion of a Q&A in this book was its universal applicability. Over the years, selected Q&A's have routinely been reprinted in books and newsletters. *Computerworld* readers tell me that particularly appropriate Q&A's frequently reappear on bulletin boards. Professors tell me that "Turnaround Time" has been a continuing source for case study material.

The book is organized into five parts, each representing a general computer/MIS topic area. These parts are management, organization, information systems, education, and careers (see the "Contents" pages for details). Within each part, the Q&A's are grouped by category (28 categories in all). Several of the more encompassing categories have subcategories. The detailed keyword index at the end of the book will also help you to find Q&A's that relate to a particular topic.

In "Turnaround Time," I've attempted to add insight, suggest an approach to a solution, identify trends, raise an issue, articulate a better way, resolve differences of opinion, question "tradition," and on occasion, bring on a chuckle. I sincerely hope that you enjoy and profit from this collection of life's vignettes.

ACKNOWLEDGMENTS

First and foremost, I would like to thank the many people who felt that my responses were worthy of the time they spent articulating their hopes, fears, problems, concerns, and wisdom. I am truly indebted to my wife, Nancy, and Andy Kreutzer for their valuable prepublication feedback on my responses to

"Turnaround Time" correspondents. Also, I would like to thank Karl Karlson and Pat Henry, my editors at Prentice Hall, for their encouragement and vision.

Larry Long

part i

Management of Computer and Information Resources

1.1 PERSONNEL

Recruiting and Interviewing

1.1.1.   Q. During the last three years we have had two directors of the DP Department. I am the Director of Personnel and am responsible for recruiting for all department head positions.

I hired both DP directors and relied heavily on input from people in the DP Department in my final evaluation of candidates. As a result, the overriding criteria became technical capability. Neither of the people hired has lived up to our expectations and we are currently searching for a replacement.

We have learned our lesson and this time we hope to look past technical capabilities and hire someone with the potential to move us forward in computer applications. Could you give us a personality profile of a successful DP manager?

A. The successful director of an information services function: commands the technical respect of his or her peers in MIS; sets a good example in attitude and work; is committed to excellence (within the constraints of reality); is committed to the corporate good; downplays the "mystique" of computers, commands presence and is comfortable in a peer relationship with top management; is innovative and generates a continuous string of ideas; is not afraid to make and stand behind a decision; is willing to get involved in risky projects; and is genuinely concerned about the welfare of those within his or her realm of responsibility.

1.1.2.   Q. A three-member executive committee, of which I am a member, has been formed to select a successor to the retiring director of our corporate computer center. We are currently reviewing resumes of applicants. The successful applicant will take charge of a department with over 55 people and a budget in excess of six million dollars.

We are looking for someone with proven management abilities and are inviting applicants from accounting, engineering, and manufacturing backgrounds as well as data processing. One of the candidates looks very promising. His experience with computers is as a long-time user of DP services. Do you think a good manager with no firsthand DP management experience can manage a large data processing department?

A. In theory, an excellent manager should be able to apply his or her skills and make the most effective use of available computing resources. In practice, good managers with limited technical expertise often fall short of expectations. The resources available to an MIS manager are people, procedures, hardware, software, and data. To tap the full potential of these resources, the successful manager must understand them, including the capabilities and limitations of available hardware and software tools. A manager who does not have a solid technical base can fall behind very quickly in such a rapidly changing environment.

I'm not saying that a former user manager cannot become a good MIS manager. What I am saying is that the person making a successful transition must be well equipped to manage all of the resources, not just people.

1.1.3.   Q. I am graduating this year and am seeking employment in information systems. During the on-campus interviews, I was invited to three companies in three different states. The plant visit formats were similar. I interviewed from four to eight people at each site, usually individually. After the interviews, however, I didn't know much about any of the companies and I'm not sure they found out much about me.

Everybody I talked to asked the same questions and gave the same information about the company. The interviewers were not prepared to answer what I considered basic questions about the job and working environment. Wat could have been exciting and informative days turned out to be rather boring.

What can I do next time to improve the situation?

A. You have the responsibility to ask those questions which support your criteria for job selection, and the company has the responsibility to answer your questions. Each of these companies had an opportunity to make a good impression and perhaps hire you—they blew it. All too often the front end of the recruiting effort on college campuses is approached with vigor, but the follow-up site visit is not well coordinated and leaves the applicant with a bad impression of the company.

Perhaps the best way to approach the problem is for me to suggest what a company can do to make a better impression and also learn more about the applicant. At a minimum, the company should prepare a printed itinerary with names, times, and places—then stick to it. Each interviewer should make it appear that he or she came to work that day just to meet you.

The company should coordinate the questions and information dissemination so that interview time is optimized. Each interviewer could be assigned one of the following topics: corporate benefits, career path development, organizational structure, or continuing education. They could also be assigned a general inquiry topic such as the applicant's academic background, technical expertise, personal interests, career goals, or the question, "why DP?"

Although more demanding on personnel time, longer sessions with two or three interviewers provide an environment for a more efficient interchange of information.

Perhaps the next company you interview will see this column and make a concerted effort to better coordinate your visit. After all, for the moment, it is a seller's market!

1.1.4.   Q. I've been an applications programmer since graduation from college three years ago. I have no complaints about my employer or supervisor, but I am having second thoughts about a career in programming.

While I am reasonably good at it and don't have anything else in mind, I sometimes wonder if I have the temperament for it. What makes a good programmer?

A. A good programmer is perceptive, patient, persistent, picky, and productive.

These are my five Ps of programming. If you are substantially lacking in any one of these areas, perhaps you should consider a career change.

Author's note: The following Q&A picks up on the five Ps of programming.

1.1.5.   Q. I heartily agree with your five "Ps" of programming; that is, a good programmer is perceptive, patient, persistent, picky, and productive.

One of my duties is to find good programming candidates. Would you share some of your experiences on how to identify people who have the five "Ps"?

A. This topic has dissertation potential. Ultimately, it boils down to an individual and some kind of subjective IF-THEN-ELSEIF-ELSE analysis. Perhaps I can offer a few suggestions.

A good way to test whether a potential candidate is perceptive and picky is for the interviewer to purposely skim over a very important topic, such as in-house training or promotion opportunities. IF the candidate continually requests clarification AND shows genuine concern about prospects for the future, THEN continue the interview. IF the candidate listens passively, THEN stop taking notes; begin discussing topics of greater interest to the candidate—such as, perhaps, television or sports.

Look for a history of self-improvement in any area, from music to computers. IF the candidate periodically takes a course OR learns something extra just in case, THEN place a check in the "persistent" box, ELSE recommend the candidate to a competing firm.

When a candidate has a college degree or experience, interviewers tend to assume that the candidate has the prerequisite technical knowledge. Orchestrate the interview such that several people ask technically revealing questions. IF a candidate's credentials imply a certain level of technical expertise AND this expertise does not surface during questioning, THEN productivity may be a problem; play *Trivial Pursuit* with the candidate.

Patience is a tough personality trait to ferret out during an interview, but there seems to be a correlation between patience and an unwavering belief that something is best. IF the candidate steadfastly pronounces a particular language to be the only real language, THEN avoid discussion of your push to fifth generation languages; wish the now former candidate good luck and call a taxi.

1.1.6.   Q. We anticipate that our very small (one person) computer center will grow to three people by the end of next year. Our expanded responsibilities will eliminate four clerical positions.

All of these people have expressed an interest in retraining for the two new DP positions. Prior to the announcement of the personnel changes, their interest in DP was lukewarm at best.

I feel an obligation to hire from within if possible. Three years ago, I was a bookkeeper and had no background in DP. My problem: How do I pick which ones to train for the new positions? Is there any way that I can determine whether or not they will be good programmers?

A. Logic aptitude tests exist that supposedly test one's ability to become a programmer. However, I am not comfortable with these tests. There are just too many exceptions: People that fail dismally may make excellent programmers and people who achieve high scores may never write a program. These aptitude tests do not reflect the all-important intangibles.

If you can delay the decision for a few months, clear it with your boss, then announce that both of the positions will be filled from these four people.

Encourage them to develop some background in the computer field. Recommend a DP fundamentals course and perhaps a programming course at a local college. Provide after-hours instruction on equipment operation and specific applications systems, then invite the DP candidates to work with you for a short period each day.

I would anticipate that at least two of them will show a genuine interest in a career change and will make the commitment. If one or none is willing to retrain, then you may have to recruit people outside the company.

Author's note: In the next Q&A someone disagrees with me on the validity of aptitude tests.

1.1.7. Q. You came out against the use of logic aptitude tests as a means of determining a person's ability to become a programmer. I disagree.

Based on my experience, I agree that as you stated, "people who fail the tests may make excellent programmers," but the other statement that "high scorers may never be able to program" is misleading. I have never known a trainee who scored high on an aptitude test who could not perform well in programmer training. In fact, I feel confident to predict that a candidate who scores well on an aptitude test and has a strong interest in the work will invariably perform satisfactorily as a production/maintenance programmer.

We went through intervals of using or not using aptitude tests, along with interviewing and examination of prior work or schooling. The change in the failure rate was well correlated with the use of the aptitude test. So, a standard programming aptitude test should be used to screen out the unsuitable applicants.

A. During the 1960s and, to some extent, the 1970s, DP staffs were created from scratch with available people, most of whom knew little or nothing about computers. With virtually nothing to go on but past performance in an unrelated field, managers turned to aptitude tests as a means of determining an employee's potential to do programming.

This was fine for that era, but today the overwhelming majority of the people being employed in computer-related jobs has some work experience or education in the field. I contend that the proper evaluation of background information is a more effective predictor of success than an aptitude test.

I liken the use of aptitude tests for screening to the use of grade point average in the screening of students for on-campus interviews. Grade point averages do not reflect personality traits, ambition, and enthusiasm. Neither do aptitude tests.

1.1.8. Q. Would you recommend special consideration in recruiting MIS personnel?

Except for an occasional opening in another area, the bulk of our company's white-collar hiring is in data processing. Recruiting good people is tough enough without the red tape of the personnel department.

We have lost several good prospects because of delays of up to five weeks in processing an offer. Do other MIS departments do their own recruiting and hiring?

A. Full-time MIS recruiters are common in companies that hire 25 or more MIS personnel a year. Some smaller MIS departments also handle the recruiting function, primarily because of the technical nature of the positions involved.

If nothing can be done to improve the service and turnaround in the personnel department, then you should take whatever action is required to absorb the function within your department. Good people are simply not willing to wait five weeks for a response.

1.1.9.   Q. The weakest of three candidates for a programming manager's job graduated from the same college as my boss, a vice president. They hit it off very well and my boss made it clear who he wanted hired. However, the choice is mine, and I feel that either of the top two candidates are far superior to my boss's choice. What would you do?

A. Don't let your boss's personal bias get in the way of your good judgment. Hire the person you believe is the best candidate.

1.1.10.   Q. I will be graduating with a master's degree and have accepted an offer of employment with a computer manufacturer and refused all others but one. I interviewed with this company six weeks ago and was told to expect a decision in two weeks. Yesterday, out of curiosity, I called for a status report. The personnel department said that the MIS division was reorganizing and that they were delaying any decisions until after the reorganization. Reorganization or not, they have 20 slots that they need filled.

I would have considered a job offer with this company earlier but certainly not now, although I am interested in seeing how long it takes them to respond. How should I respond?

A. This company has an obligation to render a quick decision on your candidacy and you have an obligation to immediately terminate negotiations after you have accepted a position. Address the letter announcing your employment intentions to the director of the MIS division. Include an informative, but not hostile, statement of your less-than-hospitable treatment. This feedback may be the most important piece of recruiting information the director will receive all year. A competent director will insure that those that follow you will not suffer the same neglect.

Compensation Strategies

1.1.11. Q. I fought for and received authorization to award salary increases to my programmer/analysts that are almost double the increases for the rest of the company. My arguments centered on raising compensation to reach parity with other employers in the region.

I had hoped that these increases would result in more highly motivated workers. I am aware of studies that show compensation on the low end of those things that motivate computer people, but the number one priority for my staff was money.

If anything, morale is lower this year than last year. Where do I go from here?

A. The results of many studies on what motivates computer people uniformly show remuneration at or near the bottom. This conclusion was confirmed by what happened in your company. Lack of pay parity may cause someone to leave one job for another, but it is not an effective motivator. In a nutshell, highly motivated people are that way because they are inherently self-motivated or they have good managers.

Besides coordinating the efforts of a group, a good manager pays attention to the individual. A good manager makes a special effort to match assignments to the skills and interest of the individual. A good manager provides real as opposed to token guidance and support in the area of career development.

While these individual activities take up valuable time, in the long run they provide a far greater contribution to the company than nitpicking memos and meetings for meeting's sake.

1.1.12. Q. I have several years of COBOL experience. I was out of programming for several years in another department but I came back. Now I see ads for programmers with 6 to 12 months of experience within a few percentage points of my salary. A year ago my project leader told me I was his highest-paid employee; some others in his group had two to three years of experience.

Obviously, I am now looking for better employment. Are there any ordinary presumptions against me, in view of my low salary? How can I counter them?

A. Your experience speaks for itself and has a market value which will be recognized by potential employers and probably by your company if they were to hire someone with commensurate skills. There are no presumptions against you.

The compression of salaries caused by the combined effect of inflation and an ongoing seller's market have forced DPers to job-hop in order to increase real income.

For the most part, corporate compensation policies have not been adjusted to accommodate the market value of the DP professional who is currently on the staff. Until corporations recognize the necessity to adjust compensation packages for high-demand professions, compression will continue to be a major contributing factor to the very critical turnover problem in data processing.

Author's note: In the next Q&A, the above correspondent takes exception to my comments.

1.1.13.   Q. I appreciated your publishing my inquiry to "Turnaround Time" several months ago. I asked whether there were any ordinary presumptions against me in my search for new employment, given that (a) I had been back in programming only a short time, and (b) I had several years of experience but was being paid as if I had no more than one year of experience.

Your response was very helpful in framing appropriate attitudes and responses during interviews. However, it was not fully informative. You stated that there were no presumptions against me, yet one prospective employer said he suspected I was leaving because I could not do the work. He asked one of my references why I did not devote my effort to succeeding in my present position.

A. Thanks for the feedback. Such comments or implications by an interviewer should be dismissed as ignorance on the part of the interviewer and are usually not representative of the company.

Any company allowing such persons access to potential employees is making a serious mistake. In a tight market, a company should play their first team in every aspect of the recruiting function. Every person on the candidate's itinerary should be there for a reason.

1.1.14.   Q. Assuming a recent DP salary survey is accurate, our salaries are on a par with industry averages. My question is: Are these salaries an accurate reflection of what DPers should be earning?

As a systems manager, my group provides services to every division in the company. User managers with approximately the same number of subordinates earn from 30 to 60 percent more than I do, but their responsibilities are much more limited. Another interesting statistic is that my staff has a higher number of years of education than any similarly sized group in engineering or accounting.

Greater responsibility over more highly skilled people results in a lower salary. It just doesn't pan out.

A. Existing DP salary levels are artificially low and salary surveys, although accurate and comprehensive, only perpetuate the unjustified differential in salaries paid to DPers and persons with commensurate responsibility and education in other fields.

There is no quick solution. The primary obstacle is corporate recognition of the scope of DP responsibilities. We are witnessing a slow but deliberate acceptance of information services professionals as a separate and equal entity to the traditional functional areas. Equality in salaries will follow.

1.1.15. Q. The salary levels of my programmer/analyst colleagues are below that of the local area, especially for experienced people. Dissatisfaction with the most recent "increases" added fuel to the fire.

Over the last few years we have been approached several times by union organizers, but have never met to discuss the possibility of unionization.

Now, however, people including myself, who have never given unions a second thought, are now beginning to talk union.

We would be interested in your opinion on the long-term effects of unionization in a DP shop.

A. Programmers and systems analysts are professionals. The performance standard for a professional is pride. Outstanding performance is not adequately rewarded in a union environment. As a result, productivity suffers and, worst of all, innovation is dampened.

You obviously have some problems that need immediate attention, but I doubt that unionization is the solution. As amazing as it may sound, I am aware of several companies whose MIS compensation package is based on erroneous data. If you have local area compensation statistics, present them through proper channels and set up a two- to three-year schedule to attain salary parity with programmer/analysts in the local area.

If management is not receptive to working towards salary parity, then I would exercise a professional's prerogative and leave.

Morale and Retention

1.1.16. Q. Many of the DP problems that you address can be attributed to the high rate of personnel turnover, a plague that is sweeping the DP industry. Although our turnover rate is not much different than that of the industry, I refuse to accept high turnover as a "given."

Our management staff has made a long-term commitment to reduce the rate of turnover. Our initial efforts centered on the compensation package, which was increased to well above local norms. In our case, high salaries were not the solution.

We can't afford another expensive failure. Perhaps you or your readers who have had success in curtailing personnel turnover would share some tried and proven solutions. This would be helpful to the whole industry.

A. Congratulations on overcoming the most formidable obstacle to personnel retention—recognition of the problem. Too often data centers accept a high rate of turnover as part of doing business. It doesn't have to be that way. I recently visited a medium-sized installation that has not lost a DP professional in over four years.

Like you, I think we can benefit from the insights of managers of DP installations who have been successful in minimizing personnel turnover. I would like to invite readers who have experienced success in retaining personnel to share their methods and approaches.

Author's note: The two Q&As that follow are in response to this Q&A.

1.1.17.   Q. The answer to everyone's turnover problem is amazingly simple—it's called "caring." I have adopted simple methods and all have proven effective (so far).

Even though I am classified as a "programming supervisor," I really have no subordinates. We are equal, we want to help each other, we work side by side, we gripe and we settle our differences through group discussion.

When I believe people need help, we all help. I go to bat for our programmers to make sure everyone is paid commensurate with their performance; salary is not an issue. I cross-train all programmers such that everyone is covered in case of emergencies. We document our work to "help out the next person." We feel pride in work well done and I make everyone aware of a good job—right up to the vice-president in charge.

I design career paths for people. When the company cannot provide a suitable career for an exceptional individual, I tell them so. I will then advise them of other job opportunities. I want the person to be happy, comfortable, and dedicated to helping others.

I give certificates on promotions, not for our files, but for their resumes. When people want vacations, I try to juggle projects so they can go without worrying about an uncompleted assignment. I give them a free day or so after big projects. I have flexible hours and each programmer is in charge of recording his or her own hours. If they put in extra hours, I encourage them to take compensatory time off later. They all know their project and when it is expected to be finished. The rest is up to them.

I arrange a three-day outing each year and we pay for it ourselves. We take our data entry staff to lunch and thank them. We help operations streamline jobs and keep lines of communication open with technical support.

When we hire new programmers, we all make an effort to help them get a start in life and teach them very good programming habits. I just held a class for systems analysts to advise them of the "new things" we can do for them. We have fun at what we do.

No department can keep up with our productivity; it's better than ever.

A. "Caring" requires an extra effort, but as your letter points out, the personal, professional, and corporate rewards more than justify the effort.

Author's note: In the next Q&A someone disagrees with this "caring" approach to the retention of personnel.

1.1.18. Q. I read with interest the "simple" solution offered in "Turnaround Time" to the problem of programmer turnover (see preceding Q&A). Obviously, the respondent is from a geographic area or an organization which offers a high degree of flexibility in personnel policy.

Unfortunately, a great many individuals involved in DP management are not provided this luxury. Certainly some of the practices are meritorious and promote an ideal working environment.

The real world involves unionized DP shops which even include supervisory personnel. Wages and salary are determined by job classification and seniority; promotions are determined by the number of qualified applicants. Such luxuries as "comp" time are prohibited by law.

The "simple" solution of "caring" is far removed from today's DP shop and is reflective of a utopian environment which relatively few can enjoy.

Alas, what ever happened to simple solutions to complex, complicated problems?

A. Your point is well taken, but many managers have more flexibility than they care to exercise. We can care, even in a union shop.

1.1.19.   Q. I manage a small credit union with eight employees, one of whom runs our computer center. I also do some work on the computer. Linda, our computer manager, has informed me that she has taken on a part-time job that will require her to work a minimum of 25 hours a week on weeknights and Saturdays. She assured me that her part-time employment will not impact her effectiveness here at the credit union. Linda has done outstanding work for us in the past and we have no rules that prohibit a second job.

Linda's work has deteriorated since she took on the second job and I have already asked our board to adopt a policy that would place reasonable limits on part-time employment.

Linda says that she needs the extra job to make ends meet. We desperately need Linda. How can I implement this new policy and retain Linda?

A. An employer, whether primary or secondary, has every right to expect a 100-percent effort from an employee. It is the rare individual that can give this kind of effort while holding a full-time position and a part-time position that requires 20 plus hours of work per week. Apparently Linda isn't one of them.

Talk frankly with Linda about her obligation to perform to the best of her ability. If Linda is as valuable as you say she is, perhaps she is underpaid. It may be that Linda can cut back at her other job if you raise her salary. If the two of you are unable to reach a mutually agreeable solution, the only long-term alternative is to release Linda and hire someone else. A company's computer operations require constant attention, perhaps more than Linda is willing to give.

1.1.20.   Q. I switched jobs from a small to a large company in order to obtain experience with large computer systems and data communications. In my ten years as a programmer I have never been so bored. What little work I am doing would be considered entry level. I am being compensated for my ten years experience but am treated like a new recruit. Is this typical of large organizations? Can I expect the situation to improve or should I start looking elsewhere?

A. I have received similar feedback from experienced professionals who have accepted employment with other companies. The "old heads" sometimes adopt a more-knowledgeable-than-thou attitude. "Since we know so much and there is so much to learn, we'll bring you along slowly."

This attitude promotes the waste of personnel resources. A ten-year professional has already been in a few fires. If anything, an experienced professional should be treated as a learned stranger and his or her expertise tapped for new perspectives and insights.

The worst thing you can do with seasoned professionals in a new job is to "bring them along slowly." This is not a good idea for recent college graduates either. My recommendations to your manager and any manager hiring experienced professionals is to give them the standard company orientation, ask their opinion initially and often thereafter, rather than throw them to the wolves. Challenges are not only more fun, but they expedite the learning process. The end result is happier employees and a more productive department.

1.1.21. Q. My responsibilities include finance, accounting, and information services. Although we have senior people in information services, other corporate people, including myself, lack confidence in the management ability of our MIS people and we are reluctant to mainstream them into other areas.

I will lose several key people unless I can present them with career advancement opportunities. Do you have any recommendations?

A. I recognize that this is an immediate problem, but it has deep roots and there is not any quick remedy. MIS people moving up the ladder sometimes sacrifice management education to maintain a high level of technical expertise. This is an unfortunate misalignment of priorities.

An expanded set of management skills should be emphasized at each level of increasing responsibility. General education should begin to emphasize management skills after the first promotion.

I would suggest that you modify any existing career development program to emphasize ongoing management education. Given the proper educational environment, an information services manager should be at least as well prepared as managers in other disciplines to move into corporate management.

As for your immediate problem, confront these people with corporate management's reservations about their ability to take on greater management responsibilities. My guess is that they will agree and be willing to work with you on a program of self-improvement.

Performance Evaluation

1.1.22. Q. I have been promoted and am faced with the task of evaluating subordinates. Would you recommend guidelines for employee performance evaluation? My company has none.

A. Performance evaluation is a "system" encompassing a range of activities which is articulated in a manager-subordinate contract that is agreeable to both the manager and the subordinate, possibly using the MBO (management by objectives) technique. Upon completion, the subordinate should confirm an understanding of the contract and the criteria upon which performance will be evaluated and promotion will be based. Subsequent performance evaluations become a farce if the subordinate is not held accountable for his or her actions. Depending on the employee's level within the organization, accountability might be based on a project plan, MBO objectives, MIS long-range plan, deadlines, milestones, and so on.

Frequency of the periodic performance reviews would range from three months for new hires to no longer than one year. For whatever reason, many MIS managers simply go through the motions of a performance evaluation. The resultant evaluations do not delineate the top performer from the mediocre performer. This is a disservice to the employee and the company.

Rate personnel in a minimum of categories and provide a support statement with each rating. Possible categories (which should be weighted) are: technical capabilities, quality of work, verbal communication skills, written communication skills, ability to interact with others, level of contribution to goals, appropriate personal qualities (e.g., initiative, imagination, flexibility, integrity).

A written report of the evaluation is critical. A manager has an obligation to let employees know where they stand. Written documentation is equally important for both promotion and termination.

1.1.23.   Q. Our company hired a consulting firm to help us implement a performance evaluation system. The data processing department was selected as the pilot. The canned procedure marketed by this firm is similar to management by objectives (MBO).

With so many forms, our paper pushers love it. But most of the managers and project leaders are very dissatisfied and literally refuse to use it. I am in the latter group.

The idea is good, but my gut feeling is that this turkey will never fly. Are you aware of any good evaluation systems? If so, where are they and what makes them successful?

A. I have been exposed to a variety of systems but surprisingly few that have been truly successful. Those that have experienced reasonable success tend to minimize paper work requirements, emphasize ongoing evaluator training, and make sure someone has responsibility for quality control.

The probability of successfully implementing any standardized procedure is inversely proportional to the square of the paper work involved. Any paper work should be simple, straightforward, and provide the evaluator plenty of flexibility. In an apparent attempt to justify the cost of the system, some commercial systems have five highly structured standardized forms where one with a little flexibility would have sufficed. Nothing will destroy a manager's interest quicker than excessive paper work, especially if he or she is not too fond of the procedure anyway.

The implementors should conduct periodic refresher training sessions on the evaluation procedure. If this is not done, the evaluations ultimately become far too individualized, and reliable comparisons between evaluations from different managers become almost impossible.

Everyone's responsibility is no one's responsibility. Someone must be in charge of ensuring quality control and consistency in the preparation of written evaluations. As you say, some managers in your company have refused to cooperate. An MBO-type system is only as good as the quality of the worst definition of objectives.

Apply these three suggestions to your existing system. It is going to take a lot of work and cooperation, but it can be done.

1.1.24.   Q. After graduation, I took a job with a computer company and just had my six-month evaluation. Overall, my performance was rated as average, but all of the discussion centered on my attitude, dress, and hair style, rather than on the actual performance of my job.

During my sales training period, everyone gave me the impression that I was progressing at an accelerated rate, so my evaluation came as a surprise.

My evaluation was essentially a reflection of what my manager thought of my appearance. I wear a coat and tie and try to be neat. He told me that being neat was not good enough and that I should invest in new clothes.

I would prefer to spend my money on other things. How can I convince him that clothes are not one of my priorities?

A. If being a successful computer salesman is one of your priorities then I would suggest that you rethink your priorities. Your manager was wrong to have downgraded your overall performance based solely on mode of dress, but he wanted to stress the importance of appearance.

Most jobs require some kind of personal concessions. Professionals that meet frequently with high-level customers and clients have found that adopting a traditional and conservative mode of dress generally yields the best results.

How you dress does not help you make a sale, but it can knock you out of the running. The idea behind conservative dress is to help minimize the possibility of unnecessary objections so that the customer or client will focus on what you have to say or sell.

1.1.25.   Q. The phrase "by the book" was coined to describe the man I work for: Be at your desk by 8:30 in the morning; take no more than one hour for lunch; and, above all, don't make waves. I have worked as a programmer analyst for the last four years and until recently I have enjoyed plenty of creative license. Now the differences in the way I work and the way my new supervisor wants me to work have resulted in a major personality clash. We don't like each other.

I am continuing to work hard and I get a steady stream of positive feedback, except from him. During a recent performance review, he rated me "poor" in five of the six performance categories. His supporting statements were laughable.

Although I would like to stay with this company for a while, this review may have destroyed my future with the company. Should I make waves and contest his evaluation of my performance?

A. If you feel that you have been wronged and you feel that you can build a solid case for a stronger performance review, by all means, use the formal grievance channels to contest the results of your review.

No performance evaluation system can factor out a rating supervisor's personal bias against a subordinate. That is why most systems have checks and balances, one of which is that your supervisor's manager has to sign off on your evaluation. Typically this signature is a rubber stamp, except when the evaluation is contested.

If your current evaluation is grossly out of line with previous evaluations and you can document the quality and quantity of your recent work, you stand a good chance of having your ratings adjusted.

Over the long term, if you expect to stay with the company, the two of you will need to negotiate a working arrangement. This will involve a compromise on both parts.

1.1.26. Q. Twelve programmers, including myself, report to a single programming manager. He was promoted from within about a year ago and has just completed his annual performance reviews. Another programmer and a good friend of mine was livid when he returned from his review. This past year he has been the superstar of the programming group, yet he was rated as average or below average in all seven categories. Since he confided in me, I told him that my review was essentially the same.

My friend, who is now looking for another job, has confided in other programmers in an attempt to determine a pattern. It turns out that other programmers received the same mediocre ratings.

I would not be so upset if I were convinced that our manager had made a genuine effort to evaluate our work. Since he never reviewed any of my work, he never offered any feedback. He manages primarily by memo and avoids face-to-face meetings whenever possible.

Some programmers are happy to still have a job, but some of us are disappointed and feel cheated. I would like to stay but am no longer motivated to do my best. How can I be assured of a fair evaluation in the future?

A. Good programmers do not always become good managers. Your manager is obviously uncomfortable in his new position. It is his responsibility to delineate between those who perform and those who do not. I am surprised that your boss's manager approved a uniform rating of the entire programming staff. Both managers are guilty of dereliction of duty.

I would certainly recommend that you discuss your concerns with your manager. If he continues to remain isolated from his people, be sure that your boss's manager is on the schedule for your exit interview.

Communication

1.1.27. **Q.** Both of our mainframe computer systems are circa 1975. We purchased three packaged systems in the late 1970s and all are in use today. Users are vocal about their dissatisfaction of our service, yet my requests to upgrade our hardware and software are denied.

Our current resources are inadequate to sufficiently service the company's computing needs. How can I convince management to loosen the purse strings?

A. I am assuming that during the last five years you have surely espoused the obvious and probably the not-so-obvious benefits of using state-of-the-art computing resources. I would suggest that you try making an analogy between your department's end product (i.e., information) and the end product of your company.

Management personnel in the manufacturing industry understand the consequences of using outdated equipment and inefficient procedures in the manufacturing processes. Inevitably, a low-quality product is produced at an inordinately high cost. When this happens, management must confront the alternatives—shut down or upgrade.

With an information services department, the alternatives are slightly different. Realistically speaking, management must rule out a shut down. The options usually boil down to continuing the status quo or to allocating funds to upgrade the department. State-of-the-art hardware and software offer greater potential to provide "quality" information. In general, companies that continue to use dated computing resources end up paying a premium price for "low-quality" information.

I would suggest that you give management concrete examples of "quality" information. Paint a vivid verbal scenario of what kind of service they can expect in a couple of years if they continue to neglect their computing resources. Those of us in the computer community know that you have to run pretty fast just to stand still, but sometimes management has to be reminded of the benefits of progress and the consequences of inactivity.

1.1.28.   Q. Two weeks ago, management pulled the two of us and another programmer/analyst away from our routine duties and assigned us 100 percent to an emergency high-visibility development project. Our manager has essentially told us not to bother him until the project is completed. The two of us view this project as a career opportunity to show what we can do. The third member of our "committee" views it as an opportunity to do some unsupervised loafing.

We are all of equal rank and no one was appointed project leader. We were given the impression by our manager that we will be evaluated equally on the overall project effort. We are on schedule and making excellent progress toward meeting the deadline, which is three weeks from now, but only because the two of us are spending nights and weekends on the project. The long hours will continue unless we can convince our third member to pull his load. Our question is, should we report his inactivity to our boss?

A. It is not your function to evaluate your peers. I would suggest that your committee request a weekly progress meeting with your manager to tap his wisdom and to invite his feedback on how the project is going. On an "emergency high-visibility project" this should be done as a matter of course, anyway. For each meeting, prepare a brief written progress report and a summary of individual activities. If your manager doesn't already know what is happening (and I'll bet he does), then he surely will by the time the project is completed.

1.1.29.   Q. Having been in DP only three years, I would be hesitant to make a generalization about all DP management, but I can certainly speak of those where I work. Actually, I get a great deal of personal satisfaction from my job as a programmer/analyst, but I do have a lot of gripes about management and my fellow workers. The one thing that bugs me the most is that no one ever says "thank you," "good job," or "keep up the good work." I have spent countless extra hours to meet a project deadline. Recently, I suggested a procedure that will ultimately save the company $20,000 a year.

Neither management or the other programmer/analysts has ever provided any positive feedback. On the other hand, I have had enough negative feedback to last a lifetime. It's frustrating and demoralizing to myself and to a number of others in the same boat.

A. Your grievance is a universal problem and not limited to DP. People should enjoy their work and DP, in my biased opinion, affords a tremendous opportunity to do so. In order to be truly fulfilled in one's occupation, there must be continuous feedback. This feedback should include the good with the bad, but it often does not. One-sided feedback will build ill feelings and probably affect productivity. *Everyone* needs to be encouraged to strive for their best effort. Criticism has been traditionally easier than praise, but giving praise is a lot more fun. Unfortunately, many people haven't ever tried so they don't know what they are missing.

Perhaps I can give you some solace. Even though he doesn't give you any positive feedback, the alert manager will usually recognize exceptional work.

Author's note: In the following letter another reader offers a few carefully chosen words on this subject.

1.1.30.   Q. The letter complaining about the lack of positive feedback sounded to me like an opportunity to remind managers that it costs them nothing to say "thank you." The cost of neglecting those two simple words can be the loss of a valuable employee.

Even though the employees may be getting a great deal of personal satisfaction from knowing they have handled a challenge well, the victory is empty when no one else appears to notice. It should be obvious that an employee's productivity will go down when he or she is demoralized and frustrated and personal satisfaction disappears once productive labor is replaced with frustration. Alert managers would do well to say thanks when they recognize exceptional work. Does anyone else remember the old rhyme which begins, "For want of a nail, the shoe was lost..."?

A. Hear! Hear! Thanks for writing.

1.1.31.   Q. After eight months my partner, Pat, and I have just completed a report which may have a significant bearing on the direction of our company's MIS function. Yesterday the inevitable happened— we were asked to give a 90-minute presentation to the executive committee. We have about four weeks to prepare. Both Pat and I are extremely pleased with the report and feel we have made a contribution.

Our supervisor has indicated that the final presentation will be the determining factor as to whether our findings are considered. The problem is that while Pat has done a super job on the report, it is widely known that Pat has had limited success in formal presentations. When not reading the transparency, Pat stares at the floor. His slow-talking monotone will start heads bobbing in four or five minutes.

I have mixed emotions about the presentation. I am better than most in formal presentations, but I would feel awkward doing the entire presentation. Pat is well aware of the problem and has left the decision up to me. How would you approach this presentation?

A. In the MIS business, presentations are a part of life and Pat should learn to cope with this facet of the job. One does not have to look at the floor or read from notes. Skills in verbal communication can be learned and developed. Pat may never be a Grace Hopper or a James Martin, but with proper preparation and practice Pat could give an adequate-to-good presentation. You have four weeks left. Work with Pat to improve presentation skills. Pick up a good book on MIS verbal communication and select important points to incorporate in your presentation. Ask a friend who is a skilled presenter for advice. Prepare an outline and begin the practice/feedback cycle. This time will be well spent, especially for Pat.

Even after the necessary skills have been developed, to be effective the presenter must gain confidence in his or her abilities. Therefore, I would suggest that you should start and end the presentation with Pat making two short presentations of 10 to 15 minutes in between. Let Pat build self-confidence and maybe next time you can split the presentation. I wish you success.

1.1.32.   Q. The director, myself, and the three other section managers have a staff meeting once a week. Only once during the last five months has it been less than two hours long. Nine out of ten of the meetings are a total waste of time. We seem to go in circles and adjourn without deciding anything. The really critical issues seem to be brushed aside without action. Do other data processing departments hold regular staff meetings? If so, with what frequency, for how long, and what do they talk about?

A. Most DP departments have staff meetings. The frequency would vary with the volatility of the department's ongoing activities. Weekly staff meetings may be too often, but they are the easiest to schedule.

Consider adopting these two fundamental guidelines for future management meetings. First, *all* five managers should attend each meeting. Cancel and reschedule it if someone cannot make it. Second, the meeting should *never* be longer than one hour. Don't waste time on details that would be more easily resolved by the parties involved.

The content is, of course, dependent on immediate, past, and upcoming problems and issues. Prior to the meeting it is your responsibility to relate to the director any matter that you would like to discuss. It is the director's responsibility to plan the meeting and prepare a written agenda. In case you haven't noticed, meetings without a list of topics to be covered tend to ramble. Periodic meetings of the management team are a good idea if properly executed, but as you say, they can be a waste of time. A group of busy professionals getting together once a week for a rap session is hard to justify.

1.1.33.   Q. We have our share of the typical DP problems but have not made any real progress towards resolving them. As a result, new projects are dying on the vine for lack of cooperation from users and for lack of coordination within DP.

The situation has not changed much in the last five years. The same people are faced with the same problems. Limited resources, unrealistic deadlines and a substantial backlog have discouraged any real positive action.

I have recently been promoted and am now a part of the decision-making group. I'm the first new member of the group in over five years.

Reluctant to communicate concerns to the other members of the management group, the rank and file have identified with me. They are depending on me to take the initiative and get the ball rolling in the right direction for the sake of the company and to keep their careers from stagnating.

Do you have any suggestions as to how to initiate this turn-around?

A. With such limited information, I am reluctant to lay out the specifics of a turnaround plan, but perhaps I can identify the major stumbling block. Your company and others in similar straits need to make the hard decisions necessary to *create the proper environment* for systems development and ongoing operation (user involvement, methodologies, planning, etc.).

Problem, and even solution, identification is not all that difficult. The difficulty comes in making the decision to commit the necessary resources. These decisions often require individual and company sacrifices and, therefore, are sometimes delayed indefinitely. This only prolongs an uncomfortable and unproductive situation.

You and your colleagues have a responsibility to make some bold (and often risky) management decisions. A recession is no time to practice status quo management.

Ask the other members of the group if they want to continue in survival mode or put priorities into perspective and get on track to more and better information services. Free up necessary resources by issuing the death certificate to projects that are "dying on the vine."

1.2 PLANNING

1.2.1.   Q. Our company is in the process of writing a long-term information system plan. This is the first comprehensive plan that we have written. Problems that we are experiencing include the format and the content of a plan. Do you have any ideas on getting started?

A. I recommend a three-phased approach to MIS long-range planning: Phase I—Preparation; Phase II—Development; and Phase III—Implementation and Maintenance. Of the three phases, Phase I is the most critical. Phase II is somewhat mechanical, and Phase III falls into place if the plan in Phase II is done correctly.

During Phase I, certain preparatory activities must be performed. Critical areas to be addressed are attitudes toward MIS planning, the design of the planning methodology, organizational considerations, education of planners and key participants, and company-wide familiarization with the role of MIS. Before taking the first step in the actual creation of a plan, top managers must recognize an explicit MIS charter and make a commitment of their time, and perhaps resources, to the planning process. Also in Phase I, you will need to have in place a document that outlines procedures and responsibilities for MIS planning.

Failure to address these Phase I activities will usually result in a failed plan.

I recommend that two documents be compiled: a strategic-level and an operational-level plan. The strategic-level plan outlines objectives and strategies in the critical computing/information resources areas of personnel, communications, applications, education, and so on. This document should be no more than 20 pages in length. The operational-level plan describes and time-phases those tasks and projects needed to realize the strategies outlined in the strategic-level plan.

An MIS long-range plan can be one of the most cost-effective projects that an organization can undertake. However, to realize its potential, you and the key players must be rowing the boat in the same direction.

Author's note: Design and Strategy for Corporate Information Services: MIS Long-Range Planning (L. Long, 1982, Prentice-Hall, Inc.) contains details of this three-phased approach to MIS long-range planning.

1.2.2.   Q. Six months ago I was promoted to a new MIS long-range planning position. During the last two months the director and I have been meeting weekly to outline the goals and objectives for our department. However, we are having trouble distinguishing between the two, and as a result, are making little progress towards developing a long-range plan.

Could you help us delineate between goals and objectives?

A. The classic approach to any planning activity is to follow this process: Compile a mission statement; identify objectives that more fully define the mission statement; state goals in terms of results; set strategies by which to accomplish the goals; then identify specific tasks that complement the strategies.

An objective might be to provide an acceptable response time to on-line users. The goal supporting this objective might be to keep response time under 1.5 seconds 95 percent of the time.

In practice, the distinction between objectives and goals becomes blurred when writing MIS long-range plans. Don't fall into the trap of arguing the distinction ad infinitum. If the objective lends itself to supporting goals (or vice versa), then make the distinction. If it does not, consider documenting the two as a single objective-oriented statement.

1.2.3. **Q.** I was moved from development work into MIS planning about 18 months ago. Since that time I have completed two MIS plans. One was operational and the other was in response to top management's request for a strategic plan for MIS.

Both have been well received in the MIS department, but top management thinks our MIS strategic plan is still too operational. I have been asked by the director of MIS to revise the last plan to emphasize strategic planning. Do you have any suggestions about how to proceed?

A. Many MIS "strategic" plans are no more than management summaries of more detailed operational plans that concentrate on new systems development, major enhancements, and hardware upgrades. Top management's response to your strategic plan indicates to me that you may have fallen into this same trap.

You may be better off starting from scratch than trying to revise the existing MIS strategic plan. At this point, top management is not going to be satisfied with a revised operational plan. They want a plan that articulates those MIS strategies that are consistent with, and complementary to, corporate objectives.

If you have not already done so, review the corporate strategic plan to see if it identifies any directions for MIS (often it does not). Invite input from corporate planners. Follow any corporate planning guidelines to the extent possible.

Keep in mind that top management wants a strategic plan that focuses on what has to be done to achieve specific results. Through a series of discussions with top management and MIS managers, derive a consensus of what the function of MIS is to be. Then set a series of strategic objectives.

In the plan, accompany each strategic objective with a brief explanation of how that objective is to be met. Each major planning area (e.g., systems, hardware, personnel, operations, communications, and so on) should be supported by at least one strategic objective.

For example, the strategic objectives for information systems planning might be to integrate existing and proposed information systems in a data base environment, and to emphasize user friendliness and distributed processing in systems design.

Finally, keep it to 20 pages or less.

1.2.4.   Q. One of your columns mentions using the "Delphi and nominal group techniques" for time, manpower, and cost estimates on DP projects. I am not familiar with these techniques and would appreciate any information or reference material you could provide on them.

A. I received a sufficient number of inquiries about these techniques to merit dedicating a column to their explanation. The versions presented are modified to better accommodate the realities of the DP environment. The amazingly simple delphi and nominal group techniques (NGT) provide a rigorous framework by which a group of persons (committee, panel, project team, etc.) can arrive at consensus opinions and/or estimates. These techniques are effective when each person in the group has knowledge of the problem or task and the ability to provide the group with the rationale for his/her opinion.

Of the two, the delphi technique is most appropriate for making time, manpower and cost estimates. The following steps describe Delphi's iterative approach:

1. *Leader presents the task and appropriate background information.*
2. *Each person submits a written estimate.*
3. *Plot estimates.* Each estimate is plotted on a linear scale for all to see.
4. *Calculate and mark the upper and lower quartiles and the median on the same scale.*
5. *Rationale for extremes explained.* Those estimators whose estimates fall in the lower and upper quartiles are asked to explain their rationale for their low or high estimates.
6. *Discussion.* The leader coordinates an open discussion.
7. *Repeat steps 2 through 6.* The dispersion of the estimates should be reduced with each iteration. The process continues until the returns for increasing the accuracy of the estimate do not merit another iteration.

8. *The estimate is the median or the mean* (as appropriate). The dispersion of the estimates is an indication of the risk involved.

Although the nominal group technique can be used for making estimates, it is more helpful in enumeration and identification of important considerations, and for setting priorities. As an example, NGT could be used to determine what to include on an MIS service request, or for setting priorities for a queue of approved MIS projects.

NGT's iterative approach is as follows:

1. *The leader presents the task and appropriate background information.*
2. *Silent generation.* Each member of the group compiles a list of pertinent considerations, items, projects, and so on. In some cases the list to be considered will be given (i.e., queue of approved MIS projects).
3. *Leader lists items for all to see.* The leader obtains one point, without discussion, from each participant in rotation until all items are exhausted.
4. *Clarification process.* If individual items are unclear to the other participants, appropriate persons are asked for explanations.
5. *Voting and ranking.* Depending upon the number of items, an odd number somewhat less than the total of the list would be selected. For example, seven might be selected for a list of 15 items. Each participant selects what they believe to be the top seven (in our case) items, then assigns a ranking to each item by starting with the extremes and working to the middle (i.e., lst, 7th, 2nd, 6th, and so on). For ease of tabulation, each person notes the ranking for each item on a separate card.
6. *Totaling the scores.* The rankings for each item are summed and listed in order for all to see (most significant first).
7. *Discussion.* The leader coordinates an open discussion.
8. *Repeat steps 5 through 7.* The process continues until it is apparent that further iterations will not significantly improve the results.

To make estimates using the NGT, the range of possible estimates becomes the items.

Reflect back on the last occasion that you were called upon to participate in a group charged with making estimates or setting priorities. In all probability yours, like so many others, was not a pleasant experience and the result was less than 100 percent acceptable. These techniques are designed to improve the plight of those in similar circumstances.

1.2.5. Q. In a *Computerworld* in-depth series you authored on MIS long-range planning, you are 99.44 percent correct in your analysis and advice. (Nobody's perfect!) But the telling remark was "MIS planning...requires a commitment of support and cooperation from all corners and levels of corporate endeavor." In the words of the Bard, "Aye, there's the rub." How then do you set the wheels of change in motion *without* corporate backing?

A great deal goes on in a corporate structure that defies analysis from the outside. It is all very well to say that the correct procedures are thus and so, but the real problem is how to implement the MIS function correctly when nobody really wants it that way: when departments ask your advice on word processing but don't take it; when users raise hell over the inadequacies of their computer facilities while comparing them favorably with systems 1,000 times faster; when upper management returns from peer-group meetings and tells us that we have more than they (which may be true, but isn't saying much).

As near as I can gather, the real problem is fear of change. Those of us who have been in the computer business for a number of years have become used to change. Not so with those classified as "users." When *we* see something better, we drop everything and hop to it. When *they* see something better, it scares them. If we force a change on them, we are asking for trouble. It is a threat to their job security and to their intelligence. "They" are everybody from the data-entry clerks to the president of the organization.

It would be much nicer, cleaner, and more satisfying to do things as you describe, but in a small organization with the political inbreeding of ours, it won't wash. When I tried to inject a commitment to "plan" (that's all, just plan) for an upgrade of administrative computing facilities into the organization's long-range plan, response to "All in favor?" was a deafening silence—just as I expected.

A. In my MIS long-range planning methodology (the first Q&A in this section), I never promised you a rose garden. MIS long-range planning is the ultimate political, procedural, and operational challenge. Even so, it can be done.

1.2.6. **Q.** I report to the director of corporate information systems. She hired me six months ago to be the manager of programming. At about the same time, she became absorbed with the idea of creating an MIS plan and assigned a senior analyst to devote half of his time to planning. Unfortunately, the resultant plan emphasizes hardware acquisition instead of systems development.

Half of my programmers are working on "hurry-up" projects and the other half have no idea what they will be working on next month. Since I have been here, the priorities change from week to week. My former employer compiled an MIS plan that provided direction for the programming effort. My boss is very proud of her new "plan," but it does not address current or future systems projects.

Without causing undo tension, how do I ask her to enhance the plan so that we have some order and purpose to our work? All of us would feel much more comfortable with a set of priorities that would enable us to at least finish what we start.

A. Tell her in the way of a status report. The report would, of course, include your concern about managing in reaction mode and your desire for better short- and long-term direction. Mention that you need this direction to effectively schedule and use the resources within your realm of responsibility.

A good MIS strategic plan is driven by information and processing needs, not by hardware needs. If, during the course of the conversation, it becomes apparent that she does not recognize this very basic planning maxim, you may need to hint that she consider a more "integrated" plan.

You will probably be putting out fires for the rest of your days if your boss refuses to broaden the scope of her planning activity. If so, I wish you the best of luck in your next job.

1.3 HARDWARE/SOFTWARE SELECTION

1.3.1.   Q. I am a partner in a small accounting firm with three other accountants and six secretaries. About every three months the same two hardware vendors stop by to discuss the advantages of purchasing a small computer. Since I am the only person who has any formal training in computers, and that's very limited, I'm the one who talks to them. Actually, the other partners have shown interest in automating some of the office activities and would like to pursue the possibility of purchasing a computer. Although no one has said anything, it's implied that I'm in charge of the selection process. Although the two vendors who have called on us have been very accommodating and appear to have a viable product, I would like to investigate other alternatives. First, is this a good idea and, second, where do I begin?

A. The computer hardware evaluation and selection has far-reaching effects on any organization and should be well planned. I am simply going to address your question of where to begin. You already have two good vendor contacts. Your next step is to determine if there are other vendors that might offer even better alternatives.

Most major mainframe manufacturers and many small computer manufacturers have equipment and perhaps support software packages that will meet your immediate needs.

For someone in your position, simply determining who to contact is no easy undertaking. I could give you a list of five vendors that I feel have viable alternatives, but that is not appropriate. Instead, I will give you a few hints on where to begin.

First, you need to identify the vendors whom you wish to contact. Look in the yellow pages under "data processing." Call a knowledgeable friend who works in the DP profession or another such firm that has a computer. Scan your trade journals for advertisements. To get a good market cross section you need feedback from three or four vendors. Send out a few requests for information (RFI) to those vendors identified in your search. The RFI is not to be confused with a request for a proposal (RFP). The RFI has the dual purpose of identifying interested vendors and providing information on the applicable hardware and software available from each vendor. Note that in order to get two positive responses you may have to send out as many as four or five RFIs. Unfortunately, some vendors will not even bother to respond to your RFI.

After the RFI (or before, depending on the extent of your DP background), you might consider retaining a knowledgeable consultant to assist you in the selection and perhaps implementation process.

This should get you started. Good luck!

1.3.2. **Q.** Our company first bought a computer in 1959. Since that time our data processing function has experienced a rapid growth in people (3 to 400) and equipment. The entire operation is centralized.

I was appointed to serve as a representative of the Accounting Division on a committee to select the hardware for decentralizing our DP operations. I am the only user on the committee.

The committee was formed two months ago. Since then, the emphasis has been on developing specifications for benchmarks. Although reasonably computerwise, I have been unable to help in the development of these highly technical specs. The committee is going around in circles trying to identify circumstances that can be used to equitably evaluate the various alternatives.

Having no previous experience in hardware selection, I would be interested in knowing if other companies devote so much time to preparing benchmarks and how much emphasis is placed on benchmarks in the evaluation process.

A. Fifteen years ago the benchmark gained tremendous popularity because one vendor's computer system could be configured like another's. Therefore, qualitative evaluations could be made relative to performance. Not so any more.

A computer system, especially in the MIS environment, is much more. complex today. With so many variables, the results will probably require an asterisk or two that negate the possibility of any real comparison. As an alternative to benchmarks, consider using performance data compiled by current users to validate the vendor's claim.

Under most circumstances benchmark results cannot be interpreted and have little real value. In the final analysis, other factors play a more vital role in the hardware evaluation and selection process. Cost, vendor reputation, service, compatibility and availability of support software are much more critical to success.

I hope that you are selecting hardware based on a comprehensive applications systems plan. It seems as though DPers often become preoccupied with hardware and find themselves developing systems to accommodate the hardware rather than selecting hardware to accommodate the systems.

1.3.3.   Q. Recently, we adopted a rather liberal microcomputer acquisitions policy. The way the policy is written, almost any microcomputer would be acceptable. We would like to amend the policy to identify micros by manufacturer and model that would be acceptable.

In the past, we have not been very successful in our selection of micros. Half of our current micro inventory is made up of micros manufactured by companies that have gone under. Do you have an insight as to what microcomputer manufacturers will remain and thrive during the next five to ten years?

A. Perhaps I can give you some food for thought. It is no secret that the future is not in single-user, stand-alone micros. Successful micro companies will focus on products that enable microcomputer networks, multiuser capabilities, and micro/mainframe links. Those continuing to emphasize single-user stand-alone operation may be in trouble.

I would anticipate that IBM clones will continue to offer alternatives with an inviting price performance as long as IBM lets them. Clone manufacturers are at the mercy of the IBM planners. Should IBM elect to do so, they could make life very difficult for manufacturers of IBM clones.

Certainly one of the keys to survival in the highly competitive microcomputer market is access to a distribution network. Several companies have their own successful networks, while others must fight for shelf space. Retailers are finding it more profitable to limit their product offerings, so shelf space is becoming increasingly difficult to come by.

During the last three years, a few companies have introduced what I would call truly innovative microcomputers, but they have experienced only marginal success in the fickle micro market. I have a hunch that the time is ripe for the micro buying community to embrace an as yet unveiled micro.

This micro may emerge from an established company or a start up company. Time will tell.

Several very large and established companies may swim in red ink for the next few years, but they will survive. Small companies unable to absorb losses while continuing their research and development efforts may be in for a rough ride. The great micro shakedown will continue through the 1980s.

1.3.4. Q. Last year we purchased three microcomputers and electronic spreadsheet software for the accounting office staff. All three micros were idle for about six months until someone decided to figure out how to use them. Since then a half dozen people in accounting, and at least as many in other offices, keep the systems tied up continuously. To alleviate this bottleneck, we decided to order three more.

Our policy on hardware acquisition has been recently revised. Now, all micro and word processing purchases must be approved by the hardware committee in the MIS department. As their first official decision, the committee denied our request. The reason given was that we had just purchased several accounting systems that would provide us with similar or better capabilities.

These systems will not be implemented for at least a year. We look forward to that, but what about now? We have three overloaded micros that have paid for themselves many times over.

The purchase of these micros is a matter of continuous debate. The committee wants to hold down the proliferation of micros within the company (we now have seven, not counting word processing equipment). Money has never been a question.

Do you think we should give up the idea of purchasing the micros or keep the issue alive?

A. I, too, am against the uncontrolled proliferation of micros and word processing equipment. However, you have an established need and an immediate opportunity to increase productivity. It sounds a little like the hardware committee is overemphasizing the proliferation issue. In so doing, they may have lost sight of the fact that for a few thousand dollars life can be made a whole lot easier for people throughout the company.

Keep the issue alive!

1.3.5. Q. Our task group has been assigned the responsibility of writing a request for proposal for the acquisition of up to 20 microcomputers and two or three minicomputers at our research and development facility. What seemed to be a simple task became difficult when we tried to describe the distinguishing characteristics of micros and minis. Could you please help us?

A. A microcomputer is any computer that you can pick up and carry, and a minicomputer is the computer just larger than a micro. Is that technical enough? Does anybody else have a better technical description? If so, I will gladly print it.

Author's note: Several readers responded but were unable to provide any further insight.

1.3.6. Q. The scope of services that we are able to offer with our present computer configuration is limited. We feel that with a larger processor and significantly greater storage capacity, we can save the company money by updating and upgrading our service potential.

We are preparing to recommend a $500K hardware upgrade to management. Any ideas on justification?

A. First of all, I do not agree with your approach to hardware acquisition. You should not purchase the hardware and then develop systems to fit the hardware. The catalyst for hardware planning should be a comprehensive application systems plan, not the other way around.

The fundamental justification for hardware acquisition is the implementation of more effective and responsive information systems; therefore, I would recommend that you concentrate your efforts on the compilation of an application systems plan. Justify the necessary commitment of resources; then select the hardware to meet those needs.

1.3.7. Q. A manager in another department purchased a couple of micros about a year ago, and he has been very successful in applying them to his department's needs. His success has gained a lot of visibility for him and his department throughout the company. Their success is the impetus behind a decision to buy 40 microcomputers for distribution to other departments. My department, Information Systems, has been placed in charge of the evaluation, selection, acquisition, and implementation process.

In a recent meeting, many of the managers expressed an interest in purchasing portable micros so they can work at home. Most of them have no experience with desktop micros. Do you think it is advisable to purchase portable rather than desktop micros?

A. I assume that you are referring to portables, the lap variety, rather than the transportables. I define a transportable as a micro that can be packaged for movement and weighs about 20 to 30 pounds. Practically speaking, these are a little heavy for frequent movement between home and office.

On the other hand, lap micros are so portable that they invite managers to include them with other briefcase items. Several available lap computers are at least as powerful as most desktop micros. The complaints that I have heard stem from the limitations of the liquid crystal flat panel display.

I would recommend that you select a compatible desktop and portable, detail the trade-offs, demonstrate the use of each, and encourage the managers to spend at least an hour interacting with each system. Then, let them make the choice.

Given that your managers understand the trade-offs, I would expect that only those who truly need portability will opt for portable micros.

1.3.8.   Q. We have outgrown our present computer system and are in the market for another. The vice president to whom I report has asked me to review alternative systems and to submit proposals from at least two vendors for final review by the executive committee. All expenditures in excess of $100,000 must be approved by the executive committee.

I solicited proposals from six vendors. Five responded, but only two met the specifications. These two were submitted for final review. Since my job description (manager of data processing) called for the "evaluation and selection of computing hardware," I submitted a written recommendation that encouraged the committee to select the more expensive alternative. I reiterated my feelings during a presentation.

The committee authorized the purchase of my second choice. It has several distinct advantages: the operating system is more versatile, greater processing capacity, more state of the art, and, perhaps most important, it costs $80,000 less. However, the installation of the system will require that modifications be made to all existing programs. The system that I recommended is compatible with our current system.

The entire DP staff consists of myself and four others. If we order a noncompatible system, we will spend most of the next year modifying programs. To date, I have refused to order a new computer system because our current staff is not adequate to meet ongoing operational, development, and maintenance demands, much less a major system conversion. Our current system is operating at capacity, but the situation will get worse if we order the approved system. Where do I go from here?

A. Present your case in dollars and cents. If tradition holds, user requests for service will hold steady or increase, with or without a new computer. Calculate the cost of the work-force augmentation needed to maintain the current level of service while modifying systems and programs to run on the new computer system. That cost may well exceed the difference in the cost of the two systems. This bottom-line approach may encourage the committee to reexamine your recommendation from a different perspective.

1.4 VENDOR RELATIONS

1.4.1. Q. Last year I chaired a committee that conducted an exhaustive search for a new computer system. Our recommendation, which appeared to offer the greatest price-performance, was accepted. The superminicomputer selected offered close to ten times the performance of our previous system.

A year later we are still waiting for delivery of some peripherals, mainframe features, and systems software that was promised five months ago. The local sales and technical support people are of no help. The sales people cannot fill out an order form properly and the technical field staff know less about the hardware and software than we do. We have gotten the runaround so many times that we now try to solve the problems ourselves.

It is apparent that we made the wrong decision, but now we are committed. What can we do to improve our relationship with the vendor?

A. Given that you are "committed" to this vendor, you must begin to work with the vendor to resolve current problems and avoid future problems. No computer vendor wants this kind of customer dissatisfaction. If the right person were to learn of your problems, the company might very well take action to rectify the situation.

Once you are convinced that you will not get satisfaction from the local office, write a letter to the national sales manager. Document every instance where you feel the vendor has acted unprofessionally or failed to live up to stated, written, or implied agreements. Such a letter will probably put a strain on your relationship with the staff at the local office, but so be it. You will either be serviced properly by the existing staff or by their replacements.

1.4.2. Q. Do vendors really ever retaliate against users?

A. I find it hard to believe that a vendor would make a conscious attempt to retaliate against a user of their product. This would be a classic case of cutting off your nose to spite your face.

Typically, the link between the vendor and a company is the marketing representative. Derogatory statements by a company representative about a particular product usually result in an increased effort by the vendor to satisfy the customer. On the other hand, a comment that reflects poorly on the marketing representative may cause the representative to unconsciously slight that account in favor of others, perhaps in retaliation.

A close examination of the clients of virtually any computer product marketing representative will surface inequities in their treatment. These inequities could be the result of any number of circumstances.

A marketing representative might retaliate against a user who discusses vendor problems with potential clients, reporters, and so on, but not likely. In fact, it has been my experience that users tend to sugarcoat the evaluation of products they use. I always temper their remarks with this in mind. When the user publicly denounces a DP product that they use, you can bet that product and/or the service is pretty bad.

Circumstances under which marketing representatives "retaliate" or slight the company may be when a user replaces some or all vendor peripherals or memory with plug-compatible counterparts; when user company personnel constantly badmouth the equipment or software product with other associates in a local area; when the DP manager refuses to accept or even consider the marketing representative's recommendations for future upgrades; when the company is locked into a particular vendor, for whatever reason; when there are no potential sales during the commission period; and finally, when the marketing representative, or the vendor, assesses the account as "more trouble than it's worth" and forgets it in hopes they will terminate their contract.

Author's note: A reader expresses a different opinion in the following Q&A.

1.4.3.   Q. If you "find it hard to believe that a vendor would make a conscious attempt to retaliate against a user of its product" (previous Q&A), I'm afraid you've been in your ivory tower too long.

Two points of relationship with Big Brother are consistent. If you give Big Brother Sales Reps a hard time, they or their boss will go to your boss with an opinion of the inadequacy of your boss's computer department and its personnel.

Also, the Big Brother "grapevine" passes along less-than-approved recommendations on applicants who give them a hard time. A "hard time" is well defined as "not agreeing 100 percent with a Big Brother sales rep."

If you cannot believe this, look into the *Computerworld* issues over the last few years related to government DP problems with Big Brother—in Delaware, Tennessee, and Arizona.

A sales rep of any company is a "consultant" who has not one iota of responsibility for systems, programming or operations. And, of course, the user never does what the "consultant" had planned.

I have had personal experiences with Big Brother on both sides of the fence and can assure you that I am not a lone individual in this case, nor am I conducting a personal vendetta against Big Brother.

I am grateful to them for the tremendous development in the computer area over the last 30 years. There are, and have been, several other computer companies with excellent hardware and even better software, but Big Brother was the super merchandiser who got the job done. In my opinion, lacking their push over the last 25 years, this country, and many related Big Brother companies, would not be nearly as advanced as we are now.

I am a Big Brother user, but 100 percent through third-party leasing and third-party maintenance.

A. My initial remark, which you so aptly quoted, and supporting statements (see previous Q&A) were applicable to all vendors of DP products and services.

I heartily concur with the realities of retaliation, but these retaliations are prompted by circumstances discussed in the previous column and through the initiative of the individual marketing representatives and, in rare cases, their immediate managers. Vendor retaliation is accomplished without the knowledge and certainly without the support of higher-level corporate officials.

Users experiencing poor service or blatant retaliation have an obligation to circumvent the marketing representative and communicate directly with the branch manager. If the attitude of the local representatives does not improve, a letter to corporate headquarters is warranted. Corporate officers learning of such activities have an obligation to retaliate with "pink slips!"

1.4.4.   Q. For almost two years I have been the initial contact person for all hardware vendors who wish to sell us their products. By policy, all vendors are routed to me. We are a small company of 300 employees, but I still see six or seven vendors each month.

My job is to assess the compatibility of their products with existing hardware and our standards. Also, I feel an obligation to assess their knowledge of their products and their willingness to work with us towards a solution.

I am disappointed in some of the people, especially those selling word processing equipment. They are quick to tell you what others lack but cannot answer basic questions about the features of their own equipment.

Some ask "how many do you want" before assessing our most basic needs. Personally, I do not feel we should do business with these people.

When I inform one of our managers that someone will be calling on them, I usually give them my candid assessment of the salesman's capability and interest. I do this because at least half of our managers have already been sold a bill of goods, and bought hardware without regard to application. Do you feel my extra comments are appropriate?

A. Since your company's management has such a bad track record for acquisition decisions, your comments are appropriate and probably appreciated, as long as they have substance and can be substantiated with fact and logical rationale.

However, it is not your place to pass judgment on a vendor because of vendor bias or a personality clash. If you continue to provide this bonus information, you should clear it with your boss.

1.4.5.   Q. After months of fruitless job hunting for a programming position, I gave up the idea of trying to work with DP equipment and started selling it. Therefore, to all those companies which would not even grant me the courtesy of an interview, I hope the hardware I am going to sell you this year provides countless hours of unmitigated down time, heartache, and grief.

A. That's fine, but don't forget that there is a direct correlation between the level of customer satisfaction and the size of your commission.

1.5 PRODUCTIVITY IMPROVEMENT

1.5.1.   Q. As the newly appointed Supervisor of Corporate Systems Development, I am very interested in increasing the productivity of my staff and would like to obtain information on techniques for improving programming productivity.

I would appreciate any information you might have.

A. The I-want-it-yesterday syndrome surrounding the DP activity has delayed attempts of many to increase productivity in general, and in programming specifically. But attention to a few basic concepts, tools and techniques can render enormous increases in programmer productivity.

- *Mode of program development*—benefits of interactive program development are overwhelming.
- *Choice of programming language*—match to application requirements; use state-of-the-art compilers; use fourth generation languages and application generators where appropriate.
- *DBMS*—to make programs independent of data structure.

- *System development methodology*—integrated procedures for structured analysis, design, and documentation.
- *Library of reusable code*—modules that are indexed and cataloged for easy reference.
- *Chief programmer teams*—with flexibility to relocate line programmers to priority projects.
- *Structured walkthroughs*—peer reviews to insure the accuracy and quality of the end product.
- *Scheduling*—to level workload and keep individual assignments at or above 100 percent.
- *Deemphasis on extremely efficient code*—today, a savings of two milliseconds/transaction does not merit the expenditure of two man-months of effort.
- *Recruiting practices*—all programmers are not created equal, 10 percent more salary may yield 100 percent more production.
- *Retention*—one person retained may result in a person-year of effort saved in the recruiting and training of a replacement.

Although this list is not exhaustive, it should provide a starting point for self-examination.

Author's note: My list was by no means exhaustive, but the following correspondent pointed out one major omission. Another reader (following the next Q&A) wanted me to elaborate on a few key points.

1.5.2.   Q. I thought you did a remarkably thorough job of responding in a few short paragraphs to the rather global question of how to improve programmer productivity. I must admit, though, that I was a little horrified by the omission of training as a key to improving productivity. I know from previous columns that you are a staunch supporter of staff development thorough training, and I was puzzled to find that you did not identify it specifically as a means to enhance productivity.

Here are some DP examples of low productivity that would be substantially improved through specific skills training. In the more than 15 years that I have worked in the data processing industry, I have either experienced personally or observed other programmers/project leaders in the following situations:

1. Preparing a feasibility study with no training in cost-benefit analysis techniques.
2. Interviewing users with no training in data gathering or data analysis techniques.

3. Working on an on-line systems design for the first time with a batch programming background, and no exposure to on-line systems concepts or differences.
4. Managing a project or a team with no training in project estimating, PERT/CMP, work breakdown structures, etc.
5. Managing people with no training in coaching and counseling, performance appraisals, or delegation and control.
6. Interviewing candidates with no training in recruiting techniques.
7. Designing screen formats with no training in human computer dialogue design considerations.
8. Working on a data base project with no training in data base concepts.
9. Asking users to participate in the systems design effort without training them in the systems development process.

This list could go on forever. Data processing management continues to say they don't have time to train because of their project load. Clearly they haven't yet understood the relationship between inadequate performance, budget overruns, project delays and lack of training.

The vehicle that they use to train isn't important. What is important, though, is for DP management to recognize that the use of sophisticated techniques, software, or hardware to improve performance will not work unless the DP professionals are trained to use them.

I would be interested in your thoughts about the relationship of training to productivity.

A. Thanks for reemphasizing the importance of education. Unless I am speaking or writing specifically on the topic of MIS education, I unknowingly tend to treat education as a given for the improvement of systems quality, economics, professional development, morale and productivity.

The corporation not willing to commit to an ongoing and well-coordinated education program (that includes users) forfeits the opportunity to take advantage of new industry developments. These organizations are falling short of the potential of MIS—and that affects profits.

Each corporation should have at least one person, part or full time, who is responsible for MIS education. The MIS education coordinator has evolved into an integral and necessary part of the professional MIS community. The company with more than 25 MIS professionals can easily justify a full-time coordinator.

Very few of us could read through your list of examples without at least one "oops!"

1.5.3. **Q.** I read with considerable interest your response in "Turn-around Time" in reference to increasing productivity in an MIS department (the first Q&A in this section). Like most companies today, this has become a major focal point of interest to us.

We are an MIS staff of approximately 140 servicing a highly diversified two billion dollar corporation. We are currently attempting to structure a two-year comprehensive program to improve our staff's productivity, utilize a home-grown system development methodology, incorporate increased user participation and responsibility, migrate towards user nonprocedural languages and generally improve our product, timeliness of production and service, and credibility throughout the corporation.

If there are a few key points you feel might help us in our endeavors, I would be most appreciative to hear from you.

A. You are talking about a complete overhaul of corporate MIS. To realize success in such an ambitious endeavor, attention to three areas is critical: MIS long-range planning, the system development methodology, and user education.

1. Develop a comprehensive long-range plan for corporate information services. I use the word "comprehensive" to emphasize that a plan for information services incorporates not only hardware and software but policy, procedures, attitudes, people, education, and so on—all necessary ingredients of the information service function.

2. Relative to the system development methodology:
   a. Integrate the user into the methodology. The user is as much a part of the development process as analysts and programmers.
   b. Keep it simple. A lengthy, complex methodology will either fail or be more trouble than it is worth. A person's willingness to use the methodology is inversely proportional to its complexity. Don't cover all possible circumstances in the body of the written methodology. Give users and MIS professionals credit for being able to use their better judgment to handle exceptional cases.
   c. The scope of the methodology should include a project management system. A system development methodology provides the opportunity and the framework for development and implementation of a project management system.

3. Implement an ongoing in-house user education program at all levels of the corporation. User awareness and knowledge of DP/MIS can be the key to successful implementation of your program.

1.5.4.   Q. Computer terminals and microcomputers are now commonplace throughout the company and we order five to ten more every month. As more and more applications go on line, people with no typing background whatsoever are asked to use the computer to enter not only numeric data but text as well. In our training sessions, we find that some are frightfully slow and we wonder if you could recommend a good microcomputer-based package for interactive keyboard training.

A. I do not recommend specific hardware or software products. However, any of the major packages should prove adequate for your needs. Besides training software, you might also consider purchasing Dvorak keyboards for hunt-and-peck keyboarders who refuse to learn touch-typing skills. With 70 percent of the alpha keystrokes on the home row, a novice keyboarder can significantly increase his or her production with the Dvorak system.

Some companies have already implemented Dvorak keyboards in their word processing pools and are experiencing 50 percent plus increases in productivity. I expect that within a couple of years, we will be ordering as many Dvorak keyboards as we do QWERTY keyboards.

1.5.5.   Q. I am the software development manager for a manufacturing company with about 100 employees.

Six hundred people work in the plant and 400 work in the office or field sales. We are moving rapidly towards on-line interactive systems and currently support about 200 terminals. This figure includes 20 portable terminals used by our field sales staff.

Have any statistics been compiled that reflect the average ratio of terminals to employees for the various types of industries? We would like to know where we stand with respect to our peer companies.

A. I will qualify my remarks by noting that the numbers of installed terminals is not nearly as important as the quality and availability of software and data. I am not aware of any such ratios. Most companies your size and larger do not know where their terminals are located, much less how many.

In MIS, the average ratio of workstations to programmers/analysts is approaching one to one. Based solely on my observations, I would surmise that your ratio of one to five reflects a greater use of terminals than most manufacturing companies. A one-to-five ratio may be low for insurance, banking, and other companies whose employees are primarily white collar.

The same logic that supports the one programmer/one terminal theory will soon be applicable to office workers as well.

If you weigh the cost of not having a terminal available when an employee needs it against the cost of the device, the scales are tipped heavily in favor of all office workers having their own workstation.

I would expect those companies that are aggressively developing on-line systems to approach a one-to-one ratio for office workers within a few more years. By then, the typical workstation will be a micro that can be networked or used as a stand-alone system.

1.5.6. **Q.** Over half the programmers in our office are runners, and we recently submitted a written request to install shower facilities in our office building. These facilities would enable us to use our lunch hour to run.

Do you have any productivity statistics to support our contention that people are more productive after exercise?

A. Since I have publically recommended mid-day exercise as a means of increasing productivity, I hear of more and more requests for such facilities and, unfortunately, an almost equal number of rejections.

I am starting to realize that staid, old traditions are more important than increased productivity and, therefore, increased profit.

I found no formal study that renders a well-founded productivity statistic; however, I have talked to many MIS professionals and 100 percent tell me that their substantial increases in productivity (from 25 to 90 percent) can be attributed to their lunch time exercise routines. From what I read, the Japanese have not done too badly in the productivity area and they encourage exercise.

1.6 BUDGETING AND COST MANAGEMENT

1.6.1. **Q.** I am the director of a medium-sized data processing installation. All seven functional areas use our services, but there are three primary users.

Each year DP is allocated a budget and expected to provide services, including equipment and its maintenance, to anyone requesting DP service. A typical request for service is generally incompatible with existing systems or corporate objectives, or it is simply unnecessary. As you might expect, all requests are top priority.

I have suggested that the data processing department work as an internal profit center and charge out all services. Over the years our users have been spoiled by receiving "free" services and they do not relish the prospects of having to pay for them in the future.

Are there any guidelines for when DP should convert to a charge-back system?

A. A cost allocation and control system should be implemented as soon after the creation of the data processing department as procedurally and operationally possible. Any DP installation having multiple users who vie for the same limited resources should charge users for services, hardware, and materials.

A user's perspective on development and operation of information systems changes for the better after they begin paying their own way. Inevitably, users become more involved when they incur the financial burden for their DP support. This involvement can only enhance the quality of the end product.

Accompany your recommendation for a chargeback system with suggested criteria and procedures for establishing project priorities.

Author's note: Continuing with the cost allocation theme, the next four Q&As deal with the related issues of establishing the rate structure, "memo reports," "funny money," and the prorating of equipment costs, respectively.

1.6.2.   Q. I read with interest a letter in "Turnaround Time" (previous Q&A) from an analyst who was assigned a task similar to mine: to initiate a review of the procedures currently in place; and to determine rates to charge departments within the company that would fully and fairly recover all MIS costs associated with providing their service.

Do you have any recommendations on how to address my problem?

A. The rate structure for services should ultimately yield revenues that equal costs. However, the rates are not as important as the method. If you find your present cost allocation system acceptable and easy to administer, simply revise the rate structure periodically, up or down, to maintain an equilibrium of internal funds flow.

If an evaluation yields dissatisfaction with your current procedures, consider the following in developing a new cost allocation method. Although other method attributes are important, cost recovery, understandability, and fairness are essential. A method can be unnecessarily complex and, therefore, incomprehensible to the person or department paying the bill, as well as an accounting nightmare for information services. Perhaps the most difficult attribute to embody in a cost allocation method is fairness. Attempts to be fair often result in violating the understandability precept.

To accommodate these essential attributes, I would recommend that you adopt a very simple algorithm: for example, hourly charges for professional services, a combination per-transaction charge and fixed charge for major applications, and a fixed charge for smaller application systems. By carefully scrutinizing revenues and cost via "memo" charges over a one-year period, willing managers should be able to negotiate charges to the satisfaction of all concerned.

I recognize that I'm introducing subjectivity, the need for greater personal involvement and, perhaps, a few headaches on the front end, but such a method can be understood, fair, and easily updated to ensure cost recovery. The contribution to MIS goodwill and image will more than compensate for the extra effort.

This approach would be inappropriate for the environment with a high percentage of ad hoc work.

1.6.3. **Q.** You had a letter from an MIS director concerning the establishment of a cost allocation system (the first Q&A in this section). Realizing the political implications of trying to charge people for something that used to be free, we have recommended the following procedures: Implement a cost allocation system outside of the official budget/performance system, distribute "memo" reports monthly to each of the benefiting organizations along with explanatory material explaining the additional visibility and control these functional managers would then have. After a year or so of the memo report, you may find it quite easy to make the system official.

A. I heartily concur with this approach.

1.6.4. **Q.** In a recent "Turnaround Time" column (the first Q&A in this section), you advocated the use of a chargeback system. Our users simply request an allocation of so much money and, with very few exceptions, are granted their request. If users overspend, they are notified and are reallocated enough to cover the overexpenditure.

Our users refer to their computing services allotment as "funny money." Although we try to downplay the term "funny money" and emphasize the importance of budget control, our users know that overspending has no real effect on their operation or their internal budget and, therefore, pay little attention to our chargeback system.

Have you had any experience with such systems and can they be made to work?

A. What may be "funny money" to users may very well be real dollars to the data center director who must juggle limited resources to meet the ever-changing needs of users. This method of user accounting is common in your environment (universities), where educational accounts pay with "funny money" and research accounts pay with real dollars. Research accounts make the existence of a chargeback system necessary.

In order for such systems to be effective in controlling educational accounts, rigorous guidelines must be followed when making the initial allocations to each account. Users should be penalized for loose budget control by charging real dollars for the overexpenditures. The user's pocketbook must be affected before this system will work.

I personally question the worth of any chargeback system which does not involve the transfer of real dollars, except on a temporary basis. A company in the process of converting to a chargeback system might consider the use of "funny money" as an interim step. This would provide the user with an idea of the cost of computer services and perhaps soften the effect of having to transfer real dollars to the computer center for services rendered.

1.6.5. **Q.** You stated that users should be charged for actual data processing costs (the first Q&A in this section). Our company does this by prorating the cost of a piece of equipment (divided by its expected life) among the users of that equipment. Some analysts, therefore, are hesitant about using some new efficient devices because the charge to the user will be considerably higher than using older ones that are already heavily used. Isn't this self-defeating on a company-wide basis since it would be advantageous to encourage the use of better devices? Is there a better way to prorate hardware cost?

A. The objective of a cost allocation and control system is to recover costs through efficient utilization of the corporate information services resources. New capabilities and methods are constantly changing the complexion of the resource pool. The services rate structure must be flexible enough to enable service costs to be revised to encourage an optimal use of all resources, including hardware.

1.6.6. **Q.** We get the usual grumbling about the high cost of DP services, but never any serious complaints. This is surprising because our chargeback system is grossly unfair. The algorithm hasn't been changed for ten years and favors I/O-bound batch processing and discourages on-line processing.

I've been asked to investigate what we could do to create a more equitable chargeback system. I am personally against changing anything.

Any change is bound to cause problems that don't exist now. Presently, no one is complaining bitterly. Wouldn't you agree that we should leave well enough alone?

A. Chargeback systems, like information systems, need continuous maintenance to reflect changing technologies and needs.

Update the system now or suffer a more serious backlash in the future.

1.6.7. Q. In order to be approved for development, an information systems project must yield a positive discounted cash flow over the expected life of the system. Those who make the decision are primarily interested only in the bottom line. In order to obtain the bottom line, we must translate intangible benefits into dollar savings. Presently we have very little confidence in our estimate and were wondering if you could suggest a way to convert intangible benefits into tangible savings (dollars).

   A. In times past, we were able to calculate a reasonably accurate return on investment for a simple transaction-based system. The complex integrated systems of today make significant contributions to corporate profit, but over the long term and in subtle, less visible ways. The evaluation of the merit and worth of these projects is a subjective process that requires a knowledge of the tangible costs and benefits and a thorough understanding of both positive and negative intangible benefits.

   The use of the dollar as a common denominator for *all* benefits and costs is an oversimplification of the evaluation task. The introduction of earnings figures for such intangible benefits as better customer relations or increased prestige serve only to compound the error in the bottom line. Too often the bottom line is blindly accepted as gospel when, in fact, half of the estimates are, at worst, ridiculous.

   When we reduce intangibles to dollars, in essence we substitute bad estimates for the decision maker's better judgment.

1.6.8. Q. The computer revolution is grinding to a halt in our company. Three years ago management was very enthusiastic about doing whatever is necessary to improve the availability of information. That year, the Data Processing Division was favored with the highest budget increase. Management seemed to be satisfied with what we did with the money, but yesterday I was asked to cut my budget for next year. Other department managers were told to expect modest increases.

   User demands for our services are greater than ever. The proposed budget will force us to eliminate certain existing services at a time when we should be expanding. The company is doing well, so I find it difficult to accept being singled out for a budget cut.

   Do you have any arguments that might convince management to reconsider their request? I have not approached them yet.

   A. The budgetary process is a series of negotiations that ultimately yield the optimum allocation of funds for the good of the company. All you can do at this point is present a well-documented case for getting the level of funding necessary to service the data processing and information needs of your company. In so doing, identify in writing those services that will be adversely affected by the cut. If your case is rejected, and you have not already done so, implement a chargeback system.

Any company that is large enough to have department managers should have a chargeback system for computer services. A good chargeback system will result in more efficient use of computing resources and more realistic allocation of funds.

1.6.9.   Q. Although our company is experiencing increased sales, our profits are declining. As a result, I have not received, and do not expect to receive, authorization for replacing the two programmer/ analysts that I have lost in the last four months. That's 25 percent of the DP department!

We are a batch shop and are well behind the technology, but the fact remains that the company is and will continue to be dependent on the output from DP. The problem is that management does not recognize this dependency and I fully expect the staff size to continue to dwindle.

Is there anything I can do to reverse this trend?

A. During hard times, corporate management should be turning to DP to increase productivity; instead they often cut the DP budget. This can only be attributed to their lack of awareness of what DP can do and, as you indicated, a lack of realization of the company's dependency on DP.

Before you become a one-man show, I would suggest you coordinate with your users and identify those application systems areas that could be computerized or improved in order to show a net dollar savings. Develop a benefit-cost analysis for each proposed project. Supplement these B/C analyses with discussions of all of the accompanying intangible benefits (e.g., better management information through exception reporting, improved customer relations, and so on). Present this package to management to show what can be done, then outline the resources necessary to accomplish what you propose.

As long as you continue to focus on the common good of the company, it does not hurt to be aggressive to justify your existence and future growth.

1.6.10.   Q. Where can I get information that identifies guidelines for data processing annual expenses for manufacturing organizations?

Years ago this used to be 1 percent of annual sales on an average, but I suspect this may have changed due to the more extensive manufacturing systems involvement that currently exists.

A. Statistics on the DP budget as a percent of annual sales is compiled and published regularly. The results of these surveys are interesting but have little real value.

For any given company the data needed to compute the DP budget as a percent of annual sales is readily available. However, an in-depth look at the scope of services supported by the various DP budgets would surface disparities which render existing statistics meaningless. For example, the DP budget may or may not encompass the following activities: data entry (often done at the source); hardware and/or personnel at remote locations in distributed processing environments; CAM (computer-aided manufacturing); word processing; and so on. Also, the level of sophistication is directly proportional to computing power and number of personnel and, therefore, the budget.

In order to provide useful guidelines for DP budget preparation, a budget survey must consider the variations in the scope of DP service.

1.6.11.   Q. Six months ago I hired a new director of information systems. He took over a difficult situation and has been doing very well. The steering committee has approved all of his recommendations to date, but all of us were taken by surprise when he proposed doubling his budget during the next three years, from $3 million to $6 million. He stated that this increase is needed to bring us up to parity with our peer companies.

We are seriously considering approving most, if not all, of the proposed increase. But before doing so, we would like to know if other companies are making similar commitments in an attempt to "catch up."

A. In truth, relatively few companies have adopted the giant-leap strategy in an attempt to become state-of-the-art users of computer technology, but more should. If you are way behind now, you can't catch up "gradually."

Half of all MIS departments are grossly underfunded. That is, for example, if MIS funding were doubled in these departments, the net result would be a positive contribution to the organization's bottom line. These companies, of which yours may be one, are not taking full advantage of the potential of computers.

Of course, good MIS management is a necessary prerequisite. If your new manager has a well-conceived long-range plan and you remain confident in his abilities, go for it.

1.6.12.   Q. What percent of the DP budget should be committed to DP education?

A. It would be an economic disservice to the company to commit anything less than an annual average of $6,000 (not including salary) and eight person-weeks per professional employee, and $1,000 and three person-weeks for operations personnel. Depending on the scope of the DP center's activities, the DP training budget should comprise between 10 and 15 percent (no, I didn't forget the decimal point) of the total DP budget. Because the level of sophistication of DP methods, software, and hardware is increasing at an increasing rate, I would expect DP training to comprise a larger percentage each year. A DP training budget might include salaries for DP training and career development staff, seminar fees, travel, per diem, outside instructor fees, fees for self-paced courses, printed matter, training equipment, and materials.

I realize these figures are substantially above today's norm, but most computer centers are five to ten years behind in application of state-of-the-art technology. This technology gap is partly caused by a reluctance of DP and corporate managers to emphasize DP education as part of the DP job function.

The lack of a formal DP training and career development program may be the root of a variety of DP problems, one of which is turnover. A commitment of $6,000 and eight person-weeks per year per person is not excessive when you consider two points: (1) the average cost to hire an entry-level DP professional is about $6,000, and (2) the first year of employment is usually spent in a learning mode with very little contribution to department output.

1.7 PROJECT MANAGEMENT

1.7.1.   Q. For a year and a half we have allowed all professional MIS employees the latitude to set their own working hours. The experiment was a disaster, and three months ago we returned to regular working hours. Now we have the same problems that forced us to implement flexible working hours in the first place, primarily the lack of computer time during regular hours.

Our people thoroughly abused flex hours by selecting work hours, not for the good of the company, but to accommodate their social schedules.

Circumstances dictate that we consider implementation of flexible working hours again. Perhaps this mode of operation is the lesser of the two evils. Do you have any recommendations on how we should proceed?

A. MIS is project oriented and requires a close coordination between all members of the project team and users. This coordination is not possible with team members setting their own working hours.

The implementation of flex hours is doomed to failure unless procedures are established to closely control the use of flexible hours at each level in the department. Make standard working hours the rule and provide supervisory approval of flex hours on an as-needed basis. Allow individual employees a certain number of hours at their discretion, perhaps four hours per week.

Set aside a minimum of 12 hours per week on three separate days when all employees are expected to be present (e.g., Monday, Wednesday and Friday afternoons). These times can be used for department, committee and/or project team meetings.

It's human nature to take advantage of a good thing. Flexible hours can work to the benefit of all, but they must be tightly controlled.

1.7.2.   Q. If I were to characterize the greatest deficiency at our installation, it would surely be project estimation. Do you know of any project estimating formulas with proven accuracy for various levels of programmers and analysts?

A. I am not an advocate of the use of formulas for making estimates. The key to successful project estimation, and subsequently management, is simplicity. These formulas require numerous subjective evaluations (e.g., programmer capability, system complexity, probability of completion by a certain date, and so on). Some require an estimate of lines of codes before the number of programs is known. Although the formulas provide a rigorous approach to estimation, the substantial requirement for subjective input tends to negate the effect of the rigor. The work required to produce the input and the quality of the resulting estimates do not justify the effort.

There is no secret to making good estimates. However, the proper set for good project estimating can be created by the existence of a preliminary general design (versus a concept), a system development methodology with phases and milestones, and experienced DP professionals. The design defines the scope of the project and provides the detail necessary to identify logical system modules. The methodology provides a vehicle for making intermediate estimates and gathering historical statistics. I am convinced that experienced professionals can subjectively factor in such variables as system complexity and level of programmer and analyst better than formulas.

With historical statistics, a preliminary general design and other subjective variables as input, experienced DP professionals can use the delphi and nominal group techniques (both are explained in Section 1.2, Planning) to arrive at reasonably accurate consensus estimates of time, manpower and costs.

1.7.3.   Q. I am one of six project managers in data processing. The last couple of years have been extremely frustrating for all of us because project priorities are continually changing. Just as we build momentum on one project we are told to drop everything to work on another "hot" project. Sometimes these "hot" projects must give way to other "hotter" projects. The end result is that we are not satisfying anybody. We are late with one project and end up sacrificing quality on another.

We set up project schedules based on availability of resources and resource commitments at a given point in time. Needless to say, our adherence to project schedules is almost laughable.

My manager has no say in priorities and those above him cannot make up their minds on what they want. The situation is getting out of hand. Any suggestions?

A. Your problems may be rooted more deeply than a simple lack of priority guidelines, but it's a place to start. Your manager should work with appropriate high-level functional area managers (the information systems steering committee, if you have one) to establish guidelines for the enhancement and development of business systems. Although there is not a set of guidelines applicable to all companies, the following guidelines may be of some help. These were compiled by managers from diverse organizations while participating in one of my information services management seminars.

1. If the system fails, fix it.
2. Government regulation or legal requirement.
3. Required for *significant* corporate decisions.
4. Contribution to corporate profit (savings or earnings).
5. Intangible benefits.

It should be emphasized that these are guidelines and not rules. There will inevitably be exceptions, but at least the exceptions will be assessed within a framework.

1.7.4.   Q. Our DP department has 60 analyst/programmers and we are organized into teams covering each functional area. I am a project leader and manage one of the teams.

Ever since we went to the team concept, the company philosophy has been that you work on one team at a time. Consequently, everyone has a relatively permanent team assignment. As you would expect, the workload of teams varies considerably throughout the year. I'm a little upset now. In the next two or three months everyone on our team will be working overtime, and we are still falling behind.

As I walked through the office yesterday, I noticed five or six analyst/programmers reading newspapers or talking about last night's game. Our management knows that workloads at any given point in time vary tremendously among functional teams, but they seem content with the present arrangement. Do other similarly organized DP departments experience the same inefficiency in resource utilization?

A. You are certainly not the only one, but that doesn't make it right. There is very little justification for management's inflexibility in their philosophy. This type of organizational structure is better suited for much larger computing centers where each team may have several major projects at any one time. Your department is probably too small to restrict someone to one functional area.

I'm a fan of having DP professionals assigned to more than one project (not necessarily all systems development projects). This approach has several advantages. In any project there are wait states (program output, user signoff, and so on) during which progress can be made on an alternative project. Assignment to several projects cannot only be more exciting but provide a better exposure for professional development. Also, a peripheral advantage of multiple assignments is that you have a built-in mechanism of cross-training for backup.

If you or one of your concerned colleagues is in a position to make suggestions, you might recommend that each professional person maintain an hourly activity log with five to ten preset categories. After several months, a summarization of the individual and functional area logs would highlight missed opportunities for a more efficient use of personnel. Warning: This project must be carefully controlled since there is an implied incentive to say you did when you really didn't.

If management remains inflexible in their philosophy, all is not lost. How about DP education? I can think of no DP center where DP professionals would not benefit themselves and their company by some self-study. The information systems business is so dynamic that any spare time could be well spent in study on new developments and techniques.

Nobody in the DP business wants to sit on their thumbs. DP management has a responsibility to their subordinates and to the company to insure that this does not happen.

1.7.5.   Q. Three years ago I left a job as a programming manager in a small company for a job as a project leader in a large company. My performance reviews have been excellent and I am happy with my raises.

I cooperate with several other project leaders and management to schedule projects. The problem is the project deadlines are so conservative that they encourage people to work slowly. The lackadaisical effort put forth by almost everybody (including myself) results in frequent schedule slippages, but nobody seems to care.

Before changing jobs I used to enjoy coming to work. I don't any more. The work here could be very exciting, but this slow-motion pace has become a way of life. Although I am contemplating a change of careers, realistically I cannot afford it.

Do you have any suggestions that might improve the situation here?

A. I worked my way through college as a switchman on the railroad. Foremen knew exactly how much work was expected. We would slow to a snail's pace if it appeared we might switch a few extra cars. There was certainly no effort made to set a new performance standard. This type of attitude has invaded your organization.

You know that hard work and a job well done result in a healthy and more enjoyable work experience. But sometimes people have to be shown that this is the case.

By setting an example, you can be the catalyst in the reversal of this attitude. Talk to your manager and express a willingness to quicken the pace. Invite challenging assignments. Do not overcommit beyond the capabilities of your people, but establish group and individual objectives that encourage greater productivity.

Expect some resistance for the first few months, but the vast majority of the people in this business enjoy a challenge. Provide the opportunity to meet challenges and for people to see and experience the well-earned satisfaction of meeting these challenges. I hope this experiment will give you and your colleagues a different perspective on your jobs. If it doesn't, change employers—not your career.

1.8 OPERATIONS

1.8.1. Q. Requiring programmers to be on call for production problems in the data center has caused some problems in our organization. Responding to production problems is a requirement if we are to deliver output on schedule. At the same time, we want to be sure that this effort is rewarded appropriately.

I wonder how other companies handle this problem. Who should be called for production problems? How should employees be compensated? Should an employee be told at hiring that responding to production problems outside of normal working hours is a condition of employment?

A. If programmers are routinely involved in correcting production problems, the issue is not whether a programmer should be on call for production problems. Scheduled and unscheduled production is the responsibility of operations personnel. From your letter I sense an unhealthy dependency on programmers to bail them out.

Systems and programming personnel are responsible for the implementation and maintenance of fully tested and operational software. Implied is the responsibility to supply operations with fully documented instructions on production, recovery, and restart procedures. Operations personnel should be trained and capable of handling the vast majority of production problems.

Operators should not be held responsible for correcting software logic problems in a presumably operational system. Premature implementation is the best way to keep programmers busy during weekends and off-hours shifts. If this is the case, careful attention to testing procedures should minimize or eliminate the problem.

If operations personnel cannot distinguish between software and hardware problems, training is in order.

A potential employee has the right to expect an employer to describe the scope of the job function. If responding to production problems is routine (and it shouldn't be), then it should be mentioned. If such events occur rarely, a professional has an implied responsibility to respond to production problems that cannot be resolved by capable operators.

I have and will continue to categorize programmers as professionals. This precludes extra compensation (other than a sincere "thank you") for *isolated* off-hours emergencies.

1.8.2.   Q. The industry media has given very little attention to operations personnel or to the area of operations in general. Our control group interacts with every division. We operate $5 million worth of hardware. Almost every system in the company is dependent on the operations section. Without operations, employees would not get paid, orders would not be entered, customers would not be billed, and the plant would come to a standstill.

My purpose in writing is to use your column to encourage recognition of the operations function.

A. The relationship between operations and information services is a microcosm of the relationship between information services and the corporation as a whole. Just as a lack of MIS awareness delays corporate recognition of MIS, a lack of operations awareness does the same for operations. Many MIS professionals have an erroneous perception of the scope and role of operations. Perhaps this attitude can be partially attributed to a lack of media coverage.

When compared to those on the development side of the house, the champions for the cause of operations have been silent. Their words of wisdom would not only be a welcome addition to industry journals, but provide the foundation for an awareness campaign. Recognition will follow.

1.9 CORPORATE POLITICS

1.9.1.   Q. I started work as a data center manager on January 1. I was hired only after four long interviews with the MIS director and the senior vice-president that he reports to. The major reason that I was brought in was to turn the data center around. The turnaround was the focus of our discussions during the interviews.

For six and one-half months I literally worked nonstop to do exactly that. During this period, I completed many tasks that provided a firm base for the data center to move forward.

Among these were the installation of a 24-location nationwide network, negotiations of cost-saving contracts; preparation of the budget for this year and next; justification of an operating system upgrade; technical evaluation of computer-aided design and manufacturing systems; many procedural improvements; computer, front-end, and DASD upgrades; a capacity study; and a plan for reorganization.

My six-month performance review was outstanding; yet only five weeks later on a Tuesday afternoon, I received a memo telling me that I had to complete a number of tasks by 8 AM the following Monday or else.

I completed all ten tasks by the Monday deadline, including a major benefit-cost analysis. This, however, did not stop my boss from terminating me on Friday morning of that same week.

I had been praised by the senior vice-president just a few weeks earlier.

To top it off, after convincing me to leave a good position and move to another state, my great humanitarian boss wanted to give me a total of two weeks severance pay. After much discussion, I still received only one month's pay.

I never received a good reason for my termination. I think he simply did what he had planned from the beginning—bring in someone to turn the data center around and provide technical direction, then let the person go.

A second possibility is that perhaps I did too good a job and had become a threat to the MIS director. He was extremely unsure of himself and certainly lacked the technical competence required for his position.

I am now looking for another position in this area, as we cannot afford another move. I would appreciate your opinion, and I also appreciate the chance to get this off my chest.

A. It is unlikely that your boss hired you with the intent of releasing you after the turnaround was complete. A well-ordered data center without continued good management will surely deteriorate.

I believe that your presence posed an immediate and real threat to the MIS director's job security. This type of threat is common in business, but most managers prefer the traditional approach. That is, managers make life increasingly miserable for their upstart subordinates while secretly and subtly sabotaging their integrity among top management.

Your manager's approach was a blatant deviation from tradition—he simply fired you without just cause. Even a good evaluation merits another six months, and your outstanding evaluation is a lot better than good.

1.9.2.   Q. During the past six years, I have worked my way up to manager of corporate systems. Until recently, I reported to the same boss that hired me, an executive vice-president.

I have been praised for growing with the increased responsibilities that my job required. I have never received a critical performance review or, for that matter, any constructive criticism.

I had only one computer course in college, so my computer education is mostly on-the-job training. Two years ago, management discouraged me from taking graduate courses saying that I would learn no more than I could learn on the job.

Slightly more than a year ago, I hired someone with a master's degree in business administration and two years of experience as a programmer/analyst to be one of my managers. Shortly after this person came on board, I received a memo from my boss stating that he would no longer report to me but to the president. I complained to my boss that after finally consolidating systems functions, we are fragmenting the department again.

Last month, my boss told me that a new position, called the director of MIS, has been created and will be filled by the person I had hired a year earlier. I was also told that I would report to him, and that most of the people that report to me would now report to him, and that he would report to the president.

On several occasions I have expressed my dissatisfaction with the organization to my new boss and have requested a revised job description that would demonstrate the company's desire for me to stay. To date, I have received nothing but the assurance of the director of MIS that he wants me to stay. Could you suggest a strategy from this point?

A. It appears that you may be the victim of what I call the "gopher-to-vice-president phenomenon." This phenomenon occurs with surprising frequency in every variety of business endeavor.

Here's how it works. The president selects one of the top (usually, but not always *the* top) young prospects to work directly with him or her on special projects. The gopher does a bang-up job (or the president believes this is the case) and is made an assistant to the president. The next promotion is to something like assistant VP, followed shortly thereafter by a jump to, you guessed it—vice-president.

Your current boss was simply at the right place at the right time. There are definite advantages to rubbing shoulders with people in power positions. When a president or a vice-president needs someone in a hurry, the successful candidate is often within earshot.

To be sure, the change of power could have been handled more tactfully but because of political exigencies, the situation may be irreversible. Reemphasize your concerns about your future with the company, then wait a reasonable period of time for a response.

In the interim, however, I would suggest that you update your resume, maintain good relationships with your colleagues, and adopt a strategy that you are willing to leave if the right opportunity comes along.

1.9.3.   Q. With the installation of more and more minicomputer systems, my problem must be a fairly common one: At what point does a one-person computer operations manager merit the status and benefits of executive management?

In the past five years our company has gone from a manual/accounting machine/service bureau environment to an in-house data processing department which handles all accounting and MIS requirements. Shortly we will have four minis and nine terminals.

I have advanced from accounting supervisor to director of data processing through training given me by the company and substantial efforts on my own. I have organized the entire operation from the first day of the initial conversion, recommended and installed two major equipment upgrades, supervised every software system designed and programmed by a contract software house, written major programs myself, instigated a DP Board of Directors Committee and worked with a national audit firm regarding system controls and procedures. I currently run the processing operations alone and help schedule data entry needs; I also provide liaison with vendors, the software house, company management and anyone else interested in our department.

My salary has doubled in the past five years and I have a great deal of personal freedom with regard to my schedule and the needs of the department. What I do not have is recognition of the responsibility I have assumed, a salary level equal to the 14 managers of the company, or the considerable managerial benefits enjoyed by these men. I am the only woman above the level of secretary or bookkeeper in the company.

No one else has been adequately trained to back me up in case of emergency or vacation. I am always "on call," and our area could not provide many qualified people to replace me.

I began asking through channels last January what my future with the company could be expected to be, and I am still waiting for a reasonable answer. The usual response is somewhere between "look at the opportunity and training the company has already provided you with" and "the old-guard managers would never accept you, but we'll see."

I have been with this company nearly 12 years and am not looking for greener pastures elsewhere. Still I can't help but think things are not as equitable as they should be. I have been making management-level recommendations for five years, but since the final decisions are always up to "real" managers, I feel my input has not been recognized or valued. Very simply, we are where we are (a very successful DP operation) because of my efforts.

Am I being too aggressive in wanting the recognition and benefits I have described, or is there valid cause in pursuing this? Maybe you can give me an idea if I am being unrealistic in my expectations, or if management is behind the times with regard to my position.

Thank you very much for your consideration and help.

A. A typical computer center will experience growth not only in technical sophistication but in organizational attitudes. It is apparent that your rate of growth in organizational attitudes is lagging behind that of technical sophistication.

At some point in time, executive management will recognize your contribution to the corporation and afford you the appropriate status and accompanying benefits. Unfortunately, this change of attitude is usually prompted by the occurrence of a DP-related catastrophe (i.e., your resignation) or a realization of how such a catastrophe would affect corporate operations.

I am not advocating that you use your indispensability as leverage to improve your position with the corporation. Such tactics usually backfire. However, I think it's healthy when an individual refrains from open announcements of long-term commitments. The mere implication that you are not locked in to a job forever is sufficient. Management is aware of your intent to stay and is taking you for granted.

One of the top 14 managers of any company, even General Motors, should be in information services. Through integration and coordination of corporate operations, DP can play a significant role in increasing productivity, and therefore profitability, but the full potential of DP cannot be realized until it is duly recognized as a major corporate entity.

Author's note: In the next Q&A a reader offers some advice to this respondent.

1.9.4.   Q. To the author of the letter that asks "when does a one-person operations manager merit executive management status?" (previous Q&A), I would recommend:

1. Make regular written summaries of your accomplishments (e.g., increased profits, efficiency, productivity; or, reduced costly errors, staff positions required, and so on) and send them as status reports to appropriate persons.
2. Act like you belong in management's camp. Make recommendations without waiting for requests for your opinion.
3. Several months before your next performance review, schedule a meeting with your boss to review your work and get his recommendations for future goals, and so on. Let him know you expect an increase based on your corporate contributions. If the title of manager and associated perquisites are important to you, ask for them both.
4. Begin interacting with other professionals to keep abreast of job opportunities and to boost your self-confidence to ask for what you want.
5. Be prepared to use your leverage if your boss turns a deaf ear. Leave if this happens. It will be to your advantage to find a more receptive work environment.

   A. All are good recommendations, but unless they are executed carefully, some may backfire.

Author's note: Read on for another person's response to the same Q&A.

1.9.5.   Q. The letter from the female DP manager who was single-handedly running her firm's entire DP operation without being organizationally recognized as equal to the other department heads was an extreme example of the kind of problem faced by many women in DP (see the two preceding Q&As). I would like to offer a few comments.

The woman is very clearly being taken advantage of by her superiors. Unless her firm is very small *and* located in a salary-depressed area of the country, she is probably being underpaid by at least $5,000 to $8,000 (my boss concurs with this opinion). Second, it does not seem that upper management has any intention of remedying this unless forced to do so. The facts that they have been stalling her career path queries for over a year and that she has no backup are evidence enough. Your answer, I felt, was incomplete; you told her that she was right in her feelings but neglected to offer a concrete course of action.

The strategy that I offer is three-pronged. Step 1 is to obtain an adequate backup person if at all possible. It is beyond all reason for her to be expected to be on 24-hour call; beside, there is the business adage that "to be indispensable is to be unpromotable."

It is quite possible that she will encounter resistance to step 1 from upper management. However, after an appropriate length of time (about six months), step 2 may be implemented with or without the success of step 1.

Step 2 is paraphrased from an article: "Sudden sartorial splendor, coupled with a number of long lunch hours, dental appointments, etc., is a sure way of making management sit up and take notice. They will take some action if they do not want to lose a valuable employee." This is not using indispensability as a lever; it is merely making a clear statement that the old reliable doormat will not be around forever. Since she states that she has considerable schedule freedom, this should be a very easy step to implement.

If step 2 is unsuccessful, or if she senses that management will fire her for having the temerity to ask for her due, it may be necessary to go to step 3 and change jobs. She is not "looking for greener pastures" to get out of a situation that yields low benefits and high frustration. She might be surprised by how far her level of experience can take her with a company whose attitudes are neither exploitive nor stuck in the 1930s.

I hope that this will give her some ideas on possible solutions to her problem.

A. She initially asked for a confirmation of her assessment of the situation. I concurred and offered some supporting statements. Although I do not necessarily concur, she and others with the same plight might find your recommended course of action helpful.

1.9.6. Q. Profits are down drastically and management has opted for what it felt was the most equitable solution: a 25 percent across the board cut in personnel. To MIS, this means a cut from 19 to 14. Since at least six MIS staff are actively seeking employment elsewhere, the reduction problem will solve itself.

I have asked management to maintain the current level and to authorize replacement for those who are almost certain to resign in the near future. Management has rejected both requests and is standing firm on the 25 percent cut.

With attrition and no authorization to recruit replacements we could be down to nine or ten people within three or four months.

My concern is how we will provide the same services, maintain what we have, and reduce our ever-increasing backlog of requests. Do you know of other MIS departments who have successfully coped with an across-the-board cut in personnel?

A. The state of the economy has dealt most of us a low blow. But based on my observations (not statistical evidence), the majority of companies that have been forced to cut back personnel have refrained from imposing any significant reductions on their DP departments. For the most part, the decree to MIS has been to reduce the recruiting quota.

It is necessary for you to explain to top management that you cannot do X work with 19 people and X-plus work with ten people. Unless a rational decision is made to at least maintain the status quo, certain MIS-dependent operations are going to come to a screeching halt.

1.9.7. Q. I am currently a senior programmer with a large insurance company. I have been employed in the MIS field since I graduated from college, six years ago. I realized very early that I enjoy the technical aspects of MIS—programming, creating catalogued procedures, testing, time-sharing, and so on. I disdain the "people-work" and what passes at most installations for "analysis." These activities inevitably involve one in the internal corporate politics, which I abhor most of all.

I am in my sixth job. Each move was made for the same reason— I deluded myself into believing that the new employer would allow me to remain a programmer/technician (without sacrifice in compensation) and not involve me in corporate politics. The results have been disappointing.

I am now so frustrated that I am very seriously considering leaving MIS. My friends advise against that action and suggest that I try systems programming or scientific programming. I have made several unsuccessful attempts to enter these areas, but every prospective employer wants work experience.

My employers and associates praise me as an outstanding programmer/technician. Are there organizations that would appreciate and utilize my strong technical ability and desire? At the age of 28, am I locked into a career path that I know is wrong for me? Do you suggest that I leave the MIS field?

A. There is no escape from corporate politics, in information systems or any other professional career path. Every corporation has people and, therefore, a political infrastructure. Fortunately the political infighting is less intense in some positions than others.

If you like business systems programming, forget about a switch to systems or scientific programming. There is no analyst (middleman) to serve as a buffer between programmer and politics. You would be right in the middle of it.

Seek out a company with a good system development methodology and a clear distinction between programmer and systems analyst. In this environment the analyst is the primary interface with the user (and politics) and the programmer works directly from programming specifications.

I am with you. It is disappointing that some companies encourage unwilling programmers to do analysis and unwilling analysts to do programming. We don't all have to be programmer/analysts. A person with a purely technical orientation should be able to follow a career path that encourages the maturation of his or her intrinsic skills. Both employee and employer would benefit.

Author's note: In the following Q&A, a reader addresses this problem from a different perspective.

1.9.8. **Q.** I am writing to rebut your reply to a person complaining about the inevitability of corporate politics (previous Q&A) that, as he sees it, disrupts his ability to be an effective technician. Your reply essentially acknowledged the appropriateness of the person's complaint.

I believe that the writer's attitude (which is representative of the attitudes of other computer professionals) is somewhat immature. It fails to recognize the need for people-to-people communication in the operation of a major department of company.

The process of building and installing systems (especially large ones) requires close communication among individuals with a variety of backgrounds. This communication, which often takes place between people with different points of view and different expertise, is essential to success in the systems business. This communication must include the establishment of working relationships and maintenance of open communication channels between people.

To be sure, there are many instances in which personal motivations and other inappropriate factors enter into the process. The attachment of the label "politics" to all instances of communication and issues resolution is, however, incorrect. Your reply to this person's letter essentially acknowledged the appropriateness of his attitude.

You counseled him on the criteria for proper choice of his next employer (i.e., his seventh job in six years). This person needs counseling in other areas as well. Specifically, he must learn about "politics" versus "communication," and about the need to work with, communicate with, and get along with other people in his job.

He needs to be counseled that a job change whenever he becomes unhappy with decisions that are made (for reasons he is unaware of or not in agreement with) is immature and ruinous to his career.

In my years in this field, I have met many individuals whose attitude about corporate politics is as narrow and shortsighted as that of the correspondent.

Part of the solution to the perennial "turnover problem" is greater maturity on the part of individual employees.

A. The correspondent to whom you referred disdained "people-work" largely because of the political games that people play. Given the proper environment, a good programmer can work directly from detailed specifications with minimal interaction with others. In no way did I intend to downplay the importance of interpersonal communication nor did I intend to equate politics with communication.

Your letter has some good points that need to be reemphasized periodically; however, I do not agree that the original correspondent's attitude is representative of other computer professionals. We still have our communication problems. I see evidence of the recognition of the importance of effective communication by both computer professionals and users.

This recognition is the beginning of a trend to quality information systems.

1.10 ISSUES AND CONCERNS

1.10.1.   Q. Of all the pressing problems and issues in data processing, both present and future, which one do you feel to be the most critical?

A. I would like to turn this question around and ask my readers what they feel to be the most critical data processing issues or problems. Drop me a note with your title and which three of the following issues/problems you feel are the most pressing: DP auditing, privacy, certification, personnel retention, standards and procedures, continuing education, security, DP management, user interaction, rapid increase in technology, internal image, documentation, and the ever-popular "other."

Author's note: Response to this invitation was heavy. Several Computerworld *pages were devoted to reporting the results of responses. The results are described and analyzed in the following paragraphs.*

Survey Results (Data Processing Issues and Problems)

Your responses to this inquiry about the pressing problems and issues in DP have shown that "Turnaround Time" can also be used as a vehicle for testing the pulse of the DP/computer community.

Approximately 80 percent of the responses came from management personnel in the information services area from project leaders to directors. The other 20 percent of the responses were from systems analysts, programmers, and user managers. Many of the respondents not only listed the top three issues, but also included justification for or a general comment about a particular issue. I will also take this opportunity to add a few comments of my own.

Several of the respondents mentioned that the issues and problems are highly interrelated and that a change in one will usually affect several others. This point is well taken and we should keep this in mind when defining possible alternative solutions.

Listed by more than half of the respondents, **DP education** was mentioned in the top three more often than any other issue. Ironically, not one person ranked it as the premier issue. Though not specifically mentioned by any respondent, career development is sometimes used incorrectly as a synonym for DP education. Even if this interpretation skewed the results, DP education is still a critical issue.

Rapid change in technology, DP management, and **personnel retention** ran a dead head for second through fourth, with each being ranked one by numerous persons.

A distant five and six were **standards and procedures** and **documentation,** respectively. It has always been my opinion that documentation should be incorporated as part of standards and procedures. Stacks of standardized documentation forms have little meaning if not supported by standards and procedures. Several respondents combined standards and procedures and documentation into one category, so I'm not alone. If tallied together, the combination would have topped DP education and become the top issue.

There was a significant drop in the number of mentions for the remainder of the issues. In order of importance, they were: **user interactions, privacy, security, productivity, internal image,** and **certification.**

On the importance of **DP education,** one respondent wrote:

Continuing education is for everyone: professionals, managers, and support people. Very few people are so self-directed that they seek out educational opportunities to improve their skills. Such opportunities must be brought to them, even if they aren't sure they want to participate.

We either grow or we start to slip behind. There is no standing still, yet most companies hire the best people they can find, reap the benefits of past education and experience, and provide no new knowledge to their people. This must change if a work force is to remain motivated and productive.

All DP education coordinators who submitted responses noted DP management as one of the top three problems, along with DP education. This might be an indication that DP management is not convinced of the need or worth of DP education.

One respondent noted that "DP education should also include education of user management and analyst." Another added, "When users don't understand, costs go up as the resulting software is reworked to make it acceptable."

On **rapid change in technology,** "It has caused serious problems in all areas of DP." Even with the accompanying increased potential, this rapid change is wreaking havoc in the DP industry. The rate of increase in technology is greater than that of our ability to cope with these advances in hardware and software. The gap is widening and posing an even more confusing state for the DP industry.

Several people wrote that an increase in the quality of **DP management** would have significant positive effects on many of the pressing problems in DP. The following quote is representative of several responses: "Technical people are not always pleased with the idea of becoming a manager. They need to be shown the challenges of the management function, the rewards and frustrations, and how they should evaluate a potential management opportunity. Finding appropriate first-level managers for technical areas remains a continuing problem for our industry."

Also on DP management, a respondent wrote:

> Most of the skills we need to do our job are probably taught to us. Who teaches managers how to manage? Too many companies employ the 'sink or swim' approach. Since enough managers eventually 'swim,' policy is rarely challenged, but it should be challenged. The improvement of management through specific education can lead to fewer 'drownings' with advantages for all. Good management produces the kind of working environment people often seek but rarely find.
>
> Improved DP management must also lead to a wider view of business and just how it affects the DP department. Data processing managers must think like financial people, marketing people, and support people if they are to be of maximum benefit to their organization. Formal education can help show managers how to change their perspective for everyone's benefit.

Another stated that "Although I'm part of the DP management establishment, I'm having trouble convincing the other managers that DP management is a problem in our company."

"On the average, we retain our professional people for almost three years, and that's high for the area." People stay with a particular company because they see career opportunities, enjoy their working environment, sense that they are needed, and are adequately compensated (or cannot find work elsewhere). The **personnel retention** problem is too readily accepted as a given. It is a problem only because of lack of attention to the needs of employees.

DP professionals spend an enormous amount of time developing and improving systems for virtually every functional area in the company. Unfortunately, the systems within the DP environment are often neglected. The irony is that good DP systems that incorporate **standards and procedures** and **documentation** would improve the quality of all systems in the company.

A respondent stated: "If we had any interaction, it might be a problem, but since we don't, I guess **user interaction** isn't a problem."

The **privacy and security** issues were not mentioned often. As government regulations are tightened and as more corporations recognize their vulnerability, I would expect these two issues to climb close to the top during the coming years.

On the topic of **certification**, one reader noted that: "Because of the diversified backgrounds of DP professionals and the increasing critical nature of their job function, some type of certification is going to be necessary to be able to determine whether a person has the capabilities to do a particular job."

On **productivity**, a reader wrote: "An engineering rigor must find a place in the DP organization." Another noted that: "The view that software costs must continue to rise each year must not be accepted as a law of nature."

One person didn't stop with three. He said, "But I must add a fourth to this list of problems—**company management**. They will not part with a dime for *anything* (not just DP) unless they absolutely have to."

1.10.2. Q. Several of my associates and I feel we are victims of reverse discrimination. One of our peers, a woman, was promoted to project manager ahead of us and in much less time than is usual.

None of us have anything against this woman; as a matter of fact, she is well liked and respected. However, we feel she was promoted prematurely ahead of others with greater experience.

In our opinion, she was promoted unjustly so that management could point to at least one female manager in the MIS department. Should we express our concerns to management and/or take legal action?

A. Perhaps you are a victim of reverse discrimination, or perhaps you have allowed your egos to get in the way of good judgment. We all tend to exalt our accomplishments and inflate their impact on the organization.

With the number of female MIS professionals approaching that of males, the MIS department is the last place one would expect an incident of reverse discrimination. I often find the top-ranking woman in a corporation to be associated with the information services function. To be sure, we have a long way to go before women achieve well-deserving parity in MIS, but reverse discrimination is not the answer.

If this woman was promoted unjustly, I doubt that the decision was made by the people doing the promoting, but rather by people at a much higher level. If this is the case, management has probably done their homework and will be prepared to successfully counter any legal recourse.

If the promotion criteria had nothing to do with mainstreaming women into management positions, I would imagine the most qualified person got the job. In either case, my recommendation is to do nothing, for nothing is to be gained.

1.10.3.   Q. Does age discrimination color DP hiring practices? I maintain a strong yes! How many DP employees have retired from DP departments with a pension? What has happened to those who have been unable to relocate in DP jobs? Have they just faded away?

My personal experience has sadly borne out this practice of age discrimination. Since reaching 40, I have been rowing hard up stream in vain to land a new professional-level DP job.

A recent newspaper ad was pretty blatant: "Director of Systems Development, age 27–35." Of course, management must lie about age discrimination or face federal labor charges in court.

Is there a solution?

A. Age discrimination is alive and well in the youth-oriented computer/MIS community. Here is where the problem occurs. Some senior programmers and analysts have not kept abreast of the technology. These people are making salaries that are disproportionate to their contribution. There comes a time when management can get twice the productivity for the same amount of money, and they are doing just that.

There is no easy solution. Members of the over-40 group are at a disadvantage whether they are seeking management positions or programmer/analysts positions. Companies with qualified candidates for management positions are promoting from within. Companies recruiting programmer/analysts screen out candidates whose most recent salary (candidate expectations notwithstanding) is beyond the salary ceiling of available positions.

I see two possible solutions to the problem of age discrimination in the computer/MIS fields. First, we need to create an awareness of the benefits of lateral promotions of MIS people into the functional areas. Second, we need to create career paths for more senior people such that those who wish to remain in technical positions can do so with pay commensurate with their contribution. This may mean that at some point their salary is actually reduced.

We must work on the first. The second is inevitable.

part ii

Organizing
for Effective Use
of Computing Resources

2.1 INFORMATION SERVICES — STRUCTURAL ORGANIZATION

2.1.1.   Q. Our yearly MIS budget is 2 percent of sales and comprises a substantial portion of administrative costs. Since so much has been written about the importance of organizational neutrality, I have initiated an evaluation of organizational alternatives.

I feel that our present level within the organization limits our capability to be responsive. Three years ago, I reported to the comptroller. I am still the director of MIS, but now, believe it or not, I report to an assistant comptroller.

Would you endorse a suggestion that I report to the president?

A. The only definitive statement that I can make about your particular circumstance is that no head of a corporate information services (MIS) function should ever report to an assistant comptroller.

The director of a well-organized and properly chartered centralized information services organization should be at a high level, perhaps a vice-president. The optimum level is based on scope of services, the manner and degree to which information services affect events and activities in other functional areas, and to a lesser extent, the capabilities and potential of the MIS personnel. Budget share is seldom a good indicator of corporate significance.

2.1.2.   Q. We are a small company of slightly fewer than 1,000 employees. Currently, our centralized MIS division services our four locations, all of which are in the same state. Against all of my arguments to the contrary, our steering committee voted to decentralize and has asked me to draw up a plan to accomplish the move. I feel that such a move is premature and will hinder our efforts to be responsive. Is there anything I can say or do to reverse their hasty decision?

A. There is no such thing as pure decentralization of information services. You can distribute people, hardware, software, data, and procedures but somebody has to mind the store, whether you chose geographic or functional decentralization. Is your committee suggesting that each site maintain separate data bases? Who will set standards, ensure compatibility, and establish policy?

I've long been a proponent of moving processing capability closer to those who use it, but not at the expense of integration and coordination. Approach the steering committee with a plan for what I call "centralized decentralization." That is, outline a plan that distributes computing resources according to the committee's wishes, but accompany it with an organizational structure with central authority for coordinating the information services function.

2.1.3. Q. Our data processing division is now centralized, but a board-level decision has been made to go to distributed processing. Along with seven other plant managers, I will be responsible for our own DP departments.

Our DP people have been very patient in their attempts to explain distributed processing, but I am not alone in my feelings that we are getting in over our heads. Some DP people feel this way also. Although I am not resisting the move, I just believe we are moving too fast. I wonder if others are experiencing similar feelings.

A. Distributed processing is another one of those oft-used terms that has no common meaning and, therefore, is easily misinterpreted by users and MIS professionals. This lack of common understanding often leaves unresolved the questions of "what to distribute" and "what degree of distribution would best serve the needs of the company." Input/output, processing, data storage, personnel (including management), audit and control, and planning can all be distributed to one degree or another. Ask that these issues be resolved now.

Once you have a handle on exactly what is going to be distributed and how it is going to be accomplished, you and your colleagues should feel more comfortable with the move. Usually managers faced with a similar transition of MIS operations and philosophy board one of three ships: the *Resistance*, the *Cautious Optimism*, or the *Good Ship Lollipop*. It appears that your attitude will buy you a ticket on *Cautious Optimism* and possibly success.

2.1.4. Q. I work for a small state government agency (150 people). We are in the process of splitting data processing maintenance and development into two completely separate functions.

As programmers and analysts, we are upset because we do not know who is going to be transferred, and we view it as a step in the wrong direction as far as a career move.

Do you see this as the correct way to set up a data processing department? If transferred to the maintenance section, how can we make the best of it?

A. The development of an information system is ongoing. Maintenance is simply a post-implementation extension of development. For this reason, development and maintenance should be integrated. If one follows this line of reasoning, the proposed organizational changes are indeed a step backwards.

Perhaps it is unjustified, but nevertheless, there is a stigma associated with maintenance. From a career development standpoint, professionals should be given the opportunity to participate in both development and maintenance projects.

How can you make the best of it? Keep a positive attitude and be the best programmers and analysts that you can be. Conduct periodic system reviews and anticipate user requests. This responsiveness and enthusiasm will not be overlooked when it comes to promotions and managers respecting your suggestions.

Author's note: Someone disagrees with me. Read on.

2.1.5. Q. As manager of the applications software maintenance department of a major corporation, I take exception to your comments (previous Q&A) in regard to data processing functions (maintenance and development) being separate. I have worked on both sides of the issue and am convinced that the only way to control the maintenance function is to *divorce it from development.*

A separate maintenance department lends uniformity and structure to new systems, standards, and documentation. How many DP shops have we all seen, heard, and/or read about that never quite get around to documentation? How many DP shops accomplish very little, if any, new development work because their entire staff is performing maintenance?

I feel maintenance is a unique function to be staffed by the best problem solvers available. It does not have a stigma attached to it in our environment because we have the best. These people recognize that maintenance is where the action is.

It takes a special type of person to handle the pressures and rewards of maintenance. These individuals are not merely looking for a soft data processing cubbyhole in which to write code, but a challenging career and a learning experience.

Where would you want to be when a company (any company) begins to have bottom-line problems: working in new development on the next cracker-jack whiz-bang, state-of-the-art market evaluation system *or* maintaining the accounts receivables system that monitors all monies into the corporate coffers?

A. Your argument has not convinced me to reverse my position that "maintenance is simply a post-implementation extension of development." An information system is by nature dynamic, constantly growing and maturing. A system may be implemented, but it's never finished.

There should be instilled a sense of responsibility on the part of the creators. I fear that the mere existence of a maintenance staff causes development people to be relaxed in this important responsibility.

Members of the development project team gain insight and in-depth expertise in the area of the system. Even the most competent team of maintenance personnel may never have the opportunity to acquire this overview knowledge and apply it to the maintenance function. After implementation, the documentation is transferred, but a substantial investment in system awareness stays with the development team.

Your organization has had enough foresight to push aside the "stigma." It is, however, a real career consideration and must be viewed in a broader context than your organization.

These are a few of the reasons why I believe the development and maintenance functions should be integrated.

2.1.6.   Q. I am an MIS manager in charge of all computer activity within the company. I was recently given the authority to hire two new programmers. My three systems programmers have been crying for more help and tell me that they need both slots. But as it is, my 28 programmer/analysts cannot keep up with the backlog.

Is our ratio of systems to applications programmers about right, or are we understaffed in systems programming?

A. You need to light a fire under your applications group and hire a couple of systems programmers.

2.1.7.   Q. Two years ago we were a company of 25 people; today we are over 100 and growing rapidly. I am the chief financial officer and am also charged with the responsibility for automation. However, we have no computer center and I have very little contact or knowledge of how computers are used outside of accounting and finance. Each division has purchased whatever hardware and software they need to do business. As a result, we are decentralized in our use of computers. Fortunately, we have state-of-the-art hardware from a single vendor.

Our vendor has recommended that we purchase a mainframe and

centralize the information processing function. Just about everybody has told me that they like it the way it is.

Would you recommend that we move in the direction of centralization or continue as we are?

A. There is nothing wrong with decentralization as long as someone has control. However, your company may be on a one-way street to embedded, autonomous operations that will be very difficult and costly to integrate at some time in the future. It is important that you begin now to coordinate the growth of your computing resources.

I would recommend a "centralized decentralization" approach. Eventually, if not now, you will want to network your computers while maintaining decentralized operation. Work toward this goal by centralizing control of such things as hardware acquisition, software acquisition, and data management, as well as various programming, communications, and systems standards.

2.1.8.　Q. Five years ago three of us were moved from the systems division to the operations division and a technical support group was formed. We are now eight with a data base administrator and growing rapidly.

As head of the group, I report to the manager of operations, but informally receive my assignments from the manager of systems. This somewhat awkward arrangement is necessary because of the operation manager's lack of interest and knowledge of our function. My constant pleas for organizational revision have had little impact.

Is their reluctance to consider my suggestion due to some tradition or trend of which I am not aware?

A. Technical support groups have not been around long enough to form traditional patterns in functions, much less organization. If a trend exists, it is to give technical support an organizational status equivalent to systems, programming, and operations. This has been done successfully in both line and staff positions.

I would be happy to second your suggestions for an organizational revision.

2.1.9.　Q. I am currently involved in developing the structure for the use of part-time, at-home programming resources. I would be very interested in your opinion of such hiring practices and if any organizations have, now or in the past, been involved in such part-time, at-home programs.

This proposed structure is for part-time employees only. Full-time employees will continue doing program development work in the office.

A. You are one of the pioneers in an employment arrangement that I feel will be very popular in the future. At present, companies needing to supplement their programming resources rely on contract programmers. Contract programming agreements are usually between two companies. What you propose is a unique employment relationship between your company and an individual.

Companies routinely hire part-time programmers, but relatively few permit them the flexibility to work at home. Nevertheless, I think it is a grand idea whose time has come. The personality of programmers has never been 8 AM to 5 PM. And, programmers often tell me that their allegiance is more to their work than their company. A self-motivated programmer could be content and probably more productive working at home.

Having praised the possibilities of such an employment arrangement, I should speak to the practicality of implementation. I am afraid that we, as an industry, are going to have to experience the steep part of the learning curve before this type of arrangement can be a profitable reality.

A policy that permits only part-timers the flexibility to work at home will breed discontent and eventually backfire. Also, contrary to popular belief, effective programmers engage in considerable personal interaction. This means that some time must be spent on site.

Then there are the logistical, legal, and security considerations. For example, does the company provide the hardware or does it reimburse the part-timer for use of a personal workstation?

In a nutshell, I would recommend that you require that 25 percent of the work be done on site, that full-timers be rewarded for exceptional performance with a work-at-home option, that the company pay for pro rata (at $200/month) for the usage of a part-timer's workstation and telephone line, and that you set up rigorous procedures for quality control and time accounting.

2.1.10. Q. I am very much interested in the chief programmer team concept mentioned in one of your earlier columns. I would appreciate knowing more about it.

A. The team is formed to accommodate the hierarchical modular development of programs. Top-down design is paralleled in the team organization.

The basic team consists of a chief programmer, assistant chief programmer, librarian, and up to four programmers. The *chief programmer* identifies the modules (of no more than three personweeks each) in a hierarchical manner, writes the job control and "driver" program(s), and assigns and supervises the development of subordinate modules. The *assistant* or *backup chief programmer* maintains an overall knowledge of the project and does production programming. The *librarian's* functions may include maintaining the documentation library, assisting in program testing, and monitoring test file status. *Programmers* should have a range of skill levels.

Many companies have modified the team structure and member responsibilities to better suit their circumstances.

Author's note: Chief programmer teams are discussed further in the following Q&A.

2.1.11.   Q. We have a small shop with one analyst and two programmers. We work well together and each of us is involved in the maintenance and development of all our systems. Is it possible to organize as chief programmer teams with only two programmers?

A. The chief programmer team concept is most effective with teams of three to five programmers; however, you can realize some of the benefits with two-person teams. These benefits include encouraging a modular approach to program development and having a clear definition of programming project responsibility. In your case, programmer A could be the chief programmer on some teams and programmer B on others. This organization is effective even if one programmer is substantially junior to the other.

2.1.12.   Q. Currently three marketing/advertising professionals and two secretaries report to me and I have authorization to fill an empty position with another professional. The job description calls for someone with experience or a degree in marketing, but what I need is someone with a solid computer background and an interest in marketing. The personnel department refuses to change the job description because they want to retain the same complement of personnel for all product marketing managers.

My group is paving the road for other product groups in the area of microcomputer applications. However, we are beginning to get in over our heads and need help to progress any further. A couple of DP programmers have been helpful, but the time they can devote to our microcomputer needs is very limited.

Everyone in marketing, including my boss, is very impressed with what we have done, but they don't know enough about computers to understand that we are on the verge of making serious productivity gains. How do I convince my boss and the people in personnel that we need a micro specialist?

A. Tell your boss that within five years more computer specialists will work in the user areas than in centralized MIS departments. Then ask your boss if your company can afford the luxury of bucking this trend, considering that the company will miss out on opportunities for productivity gains and, possibly, opportunities to gain a competitive advantage.

Those companies that refuse to change policy or revise the organizational structure to accommodate the trend of moving technical expertise closer to the user should be preparing to "play catch up" during the next few years.

2.2 INFORMATION SERVICES—ROLES AND RESPONSIBILITIES

2.2.1.   Q. What do the following MIS professionals do: programmer, programmer/analyst, systems analyst, software engineer, systems programmer, MIS manager, EDP professional?

I am pursuing a MIS career and am unclear as to what these job titles mean.

A. The primary responsibility of most MIS organizations is the development, maintenance, and production support of computer-based information systems. Traditionally, the three dominant job titles in development and maintenance of information systems are systems analyst, programmer, and user (a person who is organizationally attached to a functional area). The production function is accomplished by operations personnel.

MIS, DP, EDP, ADP, information services, and information systems are interchangeable terms, even though subtle differences exist. Electronic data processing (EDP) has been shortened to DP with the assumption that most DP is electronic. The terms *management information systems (MIS)* and *information services* or *information systems* are more contemporary terms used to reflect an expansion of the DP function to provide information for managerial decision making.

A systems analyst, or simply analyst, is responsible for analysis, design, conversion, implementation, and evaluation of information systems. In theory the programmer designs, codes, and tests programs in accordance with specifications prepared and documented by systems analysts. Many companies prefer to combine the two functions, thus the programmer/analyst.

Software engineer is far from being an industry standard term. No two companies would describe the function of a software engineer in the same way. A software engineer could be anyone from a programmer to one who deals with systematic methods and techniques for development of information systems.

Essentially, there are two categories of programmers—applications and systems. In general, a reference to programmer implies an applications programmer. The systems programmer is concerned with the design, development, and maintenance of applications-independent software (e.g., operating systems and communications software).

An MIS manager is anyone charged with the responsibility of managing any part of the MIS function; however, the term is sometimes used to refer to the individual responsible for all corporate information services.

The bulk of practicing MIS professionals hold one of the positions you listed, but you should be aware of the other career paths that this fast-growing field has spawned. I would recommend that you call a medium-to-large company, express an interest in pursuing a MIS career, and ask if they would have time to provide you with an overview of career opportunities.

2.2.2.   Q. Personnel just informed me that they are downgrading seven of my operations people. Two are shift supervisors and the rest are operators. As is, I cannot keep anybody for more than about eight months.

Personnel says that according to their position descriptions they can justify no more than a clerical level salary. Is there anything I can do to reverse their decision?

A. In all probability, personnel is simply applying their criteria to your existing position descriptions. When was the last time you revised the position descriptions to reflect the true function and worth of your operations people?

In this volatile business, the position descriptions, like applications systems, must be continuously updated for this very reason. I am sure there are many position descriptions for operations that still reflect jobs as they were in the days of electronic accounting machines.

Author's note: The next Q&A contains some suggestions for formatting a job description.

2.2.3.   Q. Where is a good source of information for developing very specific and detailed computer operations job descriptions? I would want to include tape librarian, peripheral, console, and senior console operators.

A. I am reluctant to recommend a single source. A half dozen books present reasonable examples of classical DP position descriptions. These and other sources (primarily periodicals and other companies) can provide input, but a position description should reflect the position as it relates to your company. For example, you would think that a tape librarian position description would be straightforward, but I cannot recall two such positions with the same scope of responsibility. Although available position descriptions can provide insight, they should be used sparingly for content.

There is a danger in developing "very specific and detailed" position descriptions, especially in operations. A position description should provide enough flexibility such that persons with different titles can help one another during times of heavy activity.

If your company does not have a general format for position descriptions, the following format has a good track record:

> *position title:* rough description of duties.
>
> *position code:* for ease of accounting.
>
> *responsibility:* for MIS operational areas and other position titles.
>
> *interaction:* formal and informal interactions with persons within and external to the company.
>
> *standing committees:* those committees for which the position is a permanent or rotating member.
>
> *position requirements:* education and experience prerequisites.

2.2.4.   Q. Next month I'll be moving to another state. Although I have only ten months DP experience, I had no trouble obtaining two good job offers.

One offer is from a small company with a DP staff of only four and the other is from a larger company with a staff of over 250 in their management information services division.

I would prefer working in a small company; however, the large company offers a significantly higher salary and job security. When salary and future promotions are considered, I tend to lean toward the large company. Am I leaning in the right direction?

A. Opportunities exist in both large and small DP environments. However, these opportunities, as well as the learning experiences, are quite different. The small company offers much the same information services as the large company but on a much smaller scale. With only four people to provide these services, it stands to reason that each person must specialize in everything. In the large company you will likely become a specialist in a functional area and will probably be somewhat limited in the variety of your work assignments.

In general, the staff of a small computer center depends on breadth of knowledge for survival. The breadth of knowledge gained by working in a small company may offset the lower salary. In two years a rookie like yourself will be exposed to everything from data entry to project management. This kind of exposure would take much longer to get in a large computer center environment.

Except for the small company that is experiencing rapid growth, larger companies probably do offer more internal advancement opportunities for DP professionals. That is, you will be promoted more often—analyst, team leader, and so on.

Although I am not a proponent of one or the other, I would like to make an observation. Young people entering the DP career field tend to underestimate the value of having the broad range of experiences afforded by a small computer center.

2.2.5. **Q.** In my company you are either a programmer or a systems analyst. Each group has a manager, both of equal rank.

All new employees in management information services spend three to five years as programmers before they are "promoted" to the systems group.

I think I would enjoy systems analysis and design, but I am not cut out to be a programmer. Is programming experience really a requirement to be a good systems analyst? If so, how much is needed?

A. First, I would like to dispel the myth that the logical upgrade from a programming position is to a systems analyst position. Both are professional DP positions. Your company apparently encourages this career path and probably has systems analysts who would be better contributors as programmers and vice versa.

I have been asked this question many times and consequently have given considerable thought to a response. Though many will disagree, I would encourage people entering the data processing/information systems profession to develop at least intermediate skills in business programming. Depending on an individual's exposure to programming in college, this may take from six months to two years.

This exposure will instill an empathy for the plight of the programmer and provide background knowledge in the realities of hardware/software capabilities and limitations. These are necessary ingredients for a "good" systems analyst.

Author's note: To my surprise, the computer community stood behind me on this issue. The next letter is representative.

2.2.6. **Q.** Your response to the analyst is excellent. You have no need to apologize for encouraging DP analysts to "develop at least intermediate skills in business programming." Take it from a practitioner—it never hurts and almost always helps.

It is true that programming skills and analysis skills are not the same. But, it is also true that DP analysts without some programming knowledge are at a disadvantage in most analytical situations.

A. Thanks for your support. Your last sentence is an accurate reflection of the difference between an analyst with and an analyst without programming experience.

2.2.7.   Q. We have decided to collect all manuals and documentation and centralize them in a DP library. I promoted one of my operators to DP librarian. She will continue to report to me.
Neither of us knows very much about how to set up such a library and hope you might be able to provide some guidance.

A. I assume you already have or don't need a tape/disk librarian or an education librarian, so I will direct my comments to the "DP librarian." "Information resources librarian" might be more indicative of the function.

I would recommend that you expand your concept of the DP library to encompass DP/MIS books, relevant trade journals and periodicals, and specialized materials obtained from seminars, conferences, and vendors. These items are in addition to technical manuals, systems and program documentation, and master copies of operational and user manuals.

The librarian will be involved in all of the traditional library functions of acquisitions, cataloging, circulation, and reference. Acquisitions should just be an administrative function. Give the acquisitions budget to a library committee charged with the selection of books and periodicals. Such a committee ensures that available funds are spent on needed and current material.

The librarian should provide reference service on an ad hoc and ongoing basis. A good librarian scans material as it comes in and alerts key people to articles and books pertinent to their job functions.

The person in charge of circulation control, in our case the information resources librarian, should also be assigned responsibility for change control of systems and programming documentation.

The importance of the information resources library cannot be overstated.

2.2.8.   Q. The two people in our newly established information center and 20 programmers report to me. I am comfortable with managing programmers, but have not fared well with the two people in the information center.
Our information center has five micros and eventually it will have several terminals. Having no experience in this area, I did not know

who to hire, so I recruited one person from corporate training and the other from my programming staff.

I thought that would be the perfect combination, but I have had nothing but complaints. The programmer tries to impress people and the trainer simply cannot answer questions about the hardware or software.

What type of background is best for persons working in information centers?

A. It seems as if there are a dozen concepts for information centers. I see an information center as a place that has the tools to help users to help themselves. These tools include hardware, software, technical support, and education.

To date, no credentials package has emerged for information center personnel. In such an environment, you must have people with a solid technical base who can use and explain the use of available tools. They can come from either MIS or the user community.

After technical competence, you can look for certain desirable personality traits. People working directly with users must genuinely want them to learn so that they can eventually work independently. They must have patience and recognize that a user is not going to learn in one hour what took them years to learn.

A common failing in information centers is that support personnel would rather just do the work than show users how to do it themselves. In the long run, this is counterproductive.

2.2.9. Q. Recently, a new MIS manager was brought in from the outside. The first thing he did was reorganize the department. My organization, the systems group, remained intact, but he hired two users as business analysts. They were assigned the responsibility for needs analysis and feasibility studies, and they report directly to him. These activities were formerly my responsibility.

Neither of the business analysts has a DP background and both are continually asking my people for help. I am trying to accommodate the reorganization, but frankly, we are now spending more time on these tasks than when we did it all ourselves.

A. I am not aware of any business analysts groups with such limited responsibilities. This type of organization works well as an integrated function where business analysts complement the function of systems analysts from needs analysis through design. Why limit the involvement of the business analysts to a few activities when their expertise can be helpful in all phases of systems development?

Give the present organization three months to succeed. If it becomes apparent that the organization has failed in its present format, suggest a more integrated and extensive involvement for the business analysts.

2.2.10.   Q. Let me explain my situation. I know very little about computers and programming, but I read and enjoy *Computerworld* every week. My husband is a programming manager and he has *Computerworld* sent home rather than to his office. My husband and I seldom talk about his work, and when we do, I don't understand.

Here's the problem. It is not at all uncommon for Ralph (a fictitious name) to work two or three nights a week and often on weekends. He will work all night long at least once a month. Needless to say, his offbeat working hours not only disrupt our social, eating, and sleeping schedules, but cause a dutiful wife to wonder.

Ralph has a standard comment to any inquiry I might make. He says "It comes with the territory." Does it?

A. Yes. In the programming environment weird hours are common. There are essentially three valid reasons why a programmer would be required to work irregular hours.

First, the company computer system is usually saturated with production work during the day; therefore, off hours are used to test certain programs and systems.

Second, when something goes wrong in the machine room, the applications and/or systems programmer responsible is called, day or night.

Third, the "crisis" is unfortunately very popular in the DP environment and to meet deadlines (which are sometimes unrealistic), the programmer must work long and often frustrating nights and weekends.

2.3 USER AND MIS INTERACTION

2.3.1.   Q. Recently I was placed in charge of developing a program to improve user interactions within our corporation. I am the assistant director of what most people would consider a large information services department. During a weekly staff meeting, our systems manager suggested that I write and see what you have to say.

Here's our situation. We have the usual problems in determining what the user wants during the design phase and, consequently, our users are less than satisfied with the end products. What little feedback we get about the services we provide is routed through a vice-president who is in charge of the Information Systems Department, as well as several other corporate services. Ultimately this feedback comes to us in the form of reprimands.

In recent years we have worked very hard to develop what we consider excellent standards and procedures within the Information Systems Department. Unfortunately, the lack of interaction with functional area personnel precludes us from achieving the level of quality and service that we would like.

I would appreciate any ideas you might have that would help us improve our user relations and interactions.

A. First of all, the formal line of communication (user/DP) should not be through the vice-president. Designate one person, or more if necessary, to serve as a user liaison. This person is charged with the responsibility of rendering a level of satisfaction to the user. I am sorry to say that the user usually gets the runaround unless there is a formal communication link. A phone number and perhaps a sympathetic ear will do wonders for user relations.

Obviously a user liaison cannot solve all problems on the spot. When a compromise is the only solution, the user liaison can assist in arbitrating the differences. When no compromise is necessary, the liaison may work with the user to prepare a working plan.

Your confidence in your internal procedures indicates that you probably have a methodology for systems development and for other DP functions, such as long-range planning, and so on. Is the user incorporated in your methodologies? For example, does the project team have at least one user representative? Whether it be systems development or long-range planning for information services, the user has the right to be consulted at strategic milestones throughout the process. The user also has the obligation to provide feedback and ultimately an affirmative commitment at each of these milestones.

Several large corporations have provided slots within the organizational structure of the data center for user personnel from the various functional areas. These users return to their functional areas after one and a half to three years. This structure has several positive features. The user brings with him or her knowledge of the functional area and returns with a substantial knowledge of and sympathy for DP operations. A permanent informal communication link is established when the user returns.

I personally feel this is a good approach. However, in order to be successful, the user must voluntarily seek this assignment; therefore, the company should not only make this position attractive but provide a mechanism for mainstreaming these users back into the functional areas without impeding their careers.

There are several ways to make significant improvements in user interactions that require a minimum of effort. For example, DP professionals should make a concerted effort not to talk in computerese. Computerese may be a time saver among DP professionals, but it is not necessary to communicate with users. In addition, DP managers often fall into the trap of committing themselves to an unrealistic completion date in order to temporarily relieve tension. In the long run, this does more to impede user interaction than coming up front and telling the user the bad news.

Although the implementation of these approaches will improve user interaction, in the final analysis the key to successful user interaction is user management and analyst education. Set up an ongoing program of in-house seminars devoted to increasing awareness and knowledge in the area of information systems, department policy and procedures, and the relationships between the various functional areas. These seminars should be presented at all levels—operational through strategic. User education has evolved as the responsibility of the DP department.

2.3.2.   Q. We are in the process of writing the charter and establishing an MIS steering committee. The suggestion has been made that the existing executive committee, made up of 12 division heads, double as the MIS steering committee. Have you had any experience with this type of arrangement?

A. Yes, and it doesn't work very well. I assume that the scope of responsibility of your executive committee encompasses all phases of corporate operation, including MIS. Unfortunately, such committees often avoid the subjects of computers and information systems or give them a relatively low priority.

If done correctly, a well-written charter for the MIS steering committee will require the committee members to focus their efforts on MIS. In all probability, a select group of concerned division heads would make the best steering committee. A small working committee of five to eight high-level people can have an enormous positive influence on the direction of MIS.

2.3.3.   Q. To what extent should information services be included in corporate planning? My manager, who is the manager of information services, is usually the last to know of major corporate decisions and we are often the group that is most affected.

A. The manager/director of the corporate entity that provides information services should be a member of the executive committee (the policy-making body). The information services function has evolved to be the operational nucleus of most corporations. Whether there is a revised personnel policy, a new introduction to the product line or an opening of a new store, your boss should be aware that these changes are being considered so that their effect can be factored into information services planning.

Companies excluding data processing from the corporate management planning function are not only making the implementation of most changes unnecessarily difficult but are missing valuable input to corporate process.

2.3.4.   **Q.** I am the director of the data processing department of a $150 million light manufacturing firm. Sometimes I feel that we have an identity problem.

People refer to us as IBM (although we have had Honeywell equipment for five years), data processing, DP, and a few unmentionables. It has been many years since we have had a 407, yet I think many of the people in our company, including top management, feel we still lug around trays of cards.

What can I do to change our image and to better reflect our function?

A. To begin with, how about a department name change? The term DP denotes transaction handling. Most state-of-the-art computer centers have transcended fundamental data processing and now provide information for a more effective and efficient corporate operation and for informed management decisions.

Use the term *information* in your new name to better reflect your corporate function. Create an acronym with which people can identify. After the name change, formally announce the change via a corporate-wide memo. You and your staff should then take every opportunity to promote the new name.

As a follow-up, consider providing information systems awareness seminars for your users.

2.3.5.   **Q.** I am the liaison between my department (public relations) and our information systems group. Over the next two years we are implementing two new information systems and installing four word processing units. I meet almost daily with someone from information systems. I'm trying to learn as fast as I can, but it seems as if they revel in confusing me with jargon.

I do not want to appear uncooperative (or ignorant) and have kept my thoughts to myself. Being such a novice at this, I assume that they need to use this jargon to express their ideas. It seems to me that it would be much more convenient if they could express themselves in terms that I could understand. Do people in other companies use the same confusing jargon or do they speak in plain English?

A. By all means, mention your confusion with the continued use of jargon. In defense of your information systems friends, I doubt seriously that they are trying to befuddle you. Most do not realize the extent to which jargon, commonly called computerese, is interspersed in their casual conversation. A reminder will do wonders to not only improve the efficiency of the communication, but to the quality of the resulting system.

By being a liaison you will eventually learn some computerese through osmosis. In the meantime, you should take the initiative and develop an awareness and knowledge of computers and information processing. I am sure the education coordinator of the information systems group will be happy to steer you in the right direction.

2.3.6.   Q. I manage a small customer service group whose primary functions are order entry and responding to customer inquiries. The information for most customer inquiries is not readily available, so we normally call back the next day.

I came to the conclusion that our company is technologically obsolete in DP and is going nowhere, so we decided to order a small computer with six workstations and implement our own system. The system will enable us to be more responsible to our customers. The disadvantage of the proposed system is that it will overlap with existing processing and result in some duplicate data entry, but the benefits seem greater than the costs.

Our DP manager thinks we are wasting time and money, yet he offers no solution to our problems. Do you think we should wait on DP or proceed with our plans?

A. Information systems progress is not necessarily a function of state-of-the-art knowledge. As I talk with successful MIS and user managers, I am becoming more convinced that cooperation and willingness to learn are more important than keeping pace with the technology. Having your own system may be the answer, but before you create an essentially autonomous system, I would reestablish a dialog and an attitude of cooperation with the DP manager. Hopefully, your manager will reciprocate.

2.3.7.   Q. The work that I did in automating certain plant operations resulted in the elimination of five jobs. Ultimately 25 jobs will be eliminated. After that, we have no definite plans for further automation.

We don't anticipate any people being laid off. Nevertheless, rumors are flying that most of our 250 workers will be replaced by robots. This simply is not true, but nothing I say seems to convince them otherwise. Do you have any suggestions?

A. Our society is transitioning to an information society. The question is not whether we automate, but when and how much we automate. This is a time when management and labor must be open and frank with one another. I would suggest that you invite a labor representative to serve on the team that will evaluate any future proposals to automate plant operations. This gesture implies that labor will be fully informed of and involved in any future automation, from concept to implementation.

This may not be what plant personnel want to hear, but it may provide some small comfort. Tell them that during the next decade more jobs will be lost because of a *lack* of automation than an *implementation* of automation.

2.4 USING CONSULTANTS

2.4.1.   Q. I would be interested in your thoughts on when to use DP consultants.

A. The DP/MIS consultant should not be confused with contract programmers and systems analysts. The use of contract programmers, analysts, and other MIS professionals for work-force augmentation is an entirely different question.

The MIS consultant is most effectively used:

1. To provide specialized expertise (strategic MIS planning, networking, etc.).
2. To render new insights and different perspectives.
3. To confirm or refute a decision.
4. To aid in a specific decision-making process.

I would be remiss not to take this opportunity to comment on the use of consultants. They are underutilized by some and overutilized by others. The company struggling to maintain the status quo will invariably benefit greatly from the recommendations of a competent consultant. Unfortunately, many companies have a written or implied policy that precludes retaining consultants. In this volatile industry, no computer center can hope, nor would they want, to maintain up-to-date expertise in all facets of information services. Such policies can be stifling to corporate productivity.

At the other end of the spectrum, some companies call in consultants to assist in routine decisions and in certain less desirable activities. These companies are developing an unhealthy dependence on consultants and are forfeiting the opportunity to gain valuable internal expertise.

2.4.2.   Q. As a matter of policy, new systems development work is given to contractors even though we have 20 computer specialists on the permanent staff. Our in-house staff involvement is limited to maintenance of contractor developed systems. We probably spend more time revising these systems than it would have taken to do the development ourselves.

By the time we determine that the system is not at all what we wanted, the people that developed it are no longer available. Our users associate all this bad work with the permanent staff; therefore, we bear the brunt of just about everybody's hostilities.

While I am not in a management position, I am interested in your stand on our policy on the use of contractors.

A. This mode of use of DP contract services is common in many federal agencies and it exists to a much lesser extent in the private sector. When a DP staff exists, I would never recommend that an outside contractor be given sole responsibility for an application system. If for no other reason, the effects of the not-invented-here syndrome will significantly reduce the probability of success.

Your staff should be given the opportunity to develop functional area and technical expertise as part of your career development program. At present, this expertise is being developed by contractors.

When a DP staff exists, contractors should be used primarily for workload leveling. Even then, contractors should be integrated with existing in-house project teams. In this way, their departure does not have such a catastrophic effect on maintenance, and in-house personnel can develop the expertise necessary to be more responsive to dynamic user requirements.

It appears that user requirements were not clearly defined and communicated to your contractors. A sign-off on specifications should be SOP in any organization, especially those that use outside contractors extensively.

2.4.3. Q. We have a competent staff of information service managers, but we are highly inbred with all but one having been promoted up through the ranks. I am an Assistant Manager of Corporate Information Services for a multinational company.

I'm not alone in my feelings that we're all too close to the problems of running information services. It has been suggested that we invite fresh input from someone outside of the company, especially in the area of strategic planning. Also, we would want this individual to not only confirm or question our approaches in several other areas, but offer new insights.

Where would I find such a person?

A. Consultants with the breadth of knowledge that you desire do not confine their work to a particular geographic locale and often work on a global basis. Therefore, don't limit your search to the yellow pages.

Good consultants with a general knowledge and the wide range of DP experiences required for strategic planning are few and far between and in great demand. Such individuals often author books and articles and are invited speakers at national conferences and professional seminars. Their exposure gives you and your colleagues an opportunity to evaluate the merit of what they have to say and their potential to contribute to your organization. If you are impressed with what a particular person writes or says, the publisher or conference/seminar organizers will usually give you the consultant's business telephone number.

I would like to praise your foresight in recognizing the benefits of having ongoing input from outside the company. Invite several consultants in for at least two days each and give them an overview of information services operation, then invite their general input. Select that individual who has the most to offer and place him or her on a retainer that would include no more than two or three on-site days per month. (Consultants providing general input and advice on strategic planning tend to lose their effectiveness with too much internal exposure.)

2.4.4. Q. Our current costs for time-sharing services are in excess of $200K annually, so we have decided to move these services in-house. To help coordinate this effort, we invited proposals from three consulting firms. I am charged with evaluating the proposals and making a recommendation.

The details contained in our request for proposals were very explicit. Consequently, the scope of each proposal is about the same. What differs is the price tag.

The low bid was a fixed price from one of our time-sharing services. The high side of the two "Big Eight" estimates were about double the fixed price bid. With cost the major criteria, the obvious choice is to go with the time-sharing service. However, both Big Eight firms claim they have more experience in this area.

My boss is leaning toward the low bid even though he has not read the proposals. Any ideas?

A. Whenever you make cost the major criteria, you are asking for trouble. The cost of a service has no meaning unless it is weighed against the product's anticipated level of quality.

A common pitfall in assessing the ability of a consulting firm to perform quality work is to put too much emphasis on the company. To be sure, a company's reputation should be considered, but remember that individuals, not companies, do the work.

Ask who will be assigned primary responsibility for the project. If you intend to pay top dollar for an expert, make sure that the expert will be doing the work. If there is any question about who will be assigned to complete the project, get it in writing.

Talk with each of the proposed principals. Assess their experience, interest, and the extent of their personal commitment to the project. Frank discussions with the people expected to do the work should give you some insight into the disparity in prices and the quality of the end product.

2.4.5.   Q. I was informed last week that I will be promoted from assistant director to director of a large computer center (over 200 people). We are a solid operation but not without problems. We are very much inbred and all of our managers have been promoted from within.

In the 26 years that I have been with the company, we have never hired a consultant. Each time I mention that we might be able to benefit from the insight of someone outside the company, I am ignored by top management. The attitude both at the top and with the people in our department is that we know our company better than anybody else and can do it better if we do it ourselves. We set up a two-man planning group over three years ago and still do not have a business systems plan. We need help in planning and many other areas.

In the short term, I would like to solicit outside assistance in structured methodologies, planning, documentation, and career development. I would welcome any recommendations you might have as to how I can reverse top management's attitude about consultants.

A. Wait until you are firmly seated in the top slot and have made a couple of major decisions. Then suggest the possibility of using consultants to "enhance responsiveness to the user community."

Since consultants will be a new experience for your company, suggest a pilot project with a high probability of success and retain a proven winner to help you address this need. If you select the right project, it should be relatively easy to compile a benefit-cost analysis with very convincing numbers. A positive bottom line is always an "attention getter."

I would refrain from suggesting that consultants be retained in a variety of areas. Changes of attitude are evolutionary, not revolutionary.

2.4.6.   Q. Recently, I unknowingly created a controversy within our company when I retained the consulting arm of the company that does our auditing. The corporate controller and I evaluated several consulting firms before selecting this company to help us with the design of a consolidated accounting system.

Now three officers of the company, including the president and several division general managers, have expressed concern about a conflict of interest. Their concern was prompted when the person who manages our annual audit activity advised our controller against engaging members of his firm to do work on accounting systems.

Should we continue with the original plan or seek help from another firm?

A. Given that so many key figures are concerned and that your public accounting firm cannot present a unified front, I would recommend that you retain another firm.

I am not saying that MIS consulting and audit groups of the same firm cannot have the same client. In this situation, it is apparent that you would be fighting unnecessary battles both internally and externally.

In addition, there is a subtle point that should not be overlooked: the managing auditor lacks confidence in his firm's MIS consulting group. If he felt that they could do the job, he would have said so. I would guess that he is not willing to jeopardize his firm's bread-and-butter audit work for a one-time MIS job.

2.4.7. **Q.** A month ago I hired a consultant who professed to be an expert in microcomputers and office automation.

She just submitted a bill for $6,600 covering the first month's work—I fired her on the spot. She was to help us establish a microcomputer policy, use her technical expertise to help network clusters of microcomputers, and set up an education program to make our users more comfortable with personal computers.

She spent a lot of time on site talking with almost everyone in the company and reviewing (I think learning) our software packages. For our $6,600 she has "a good understanding of what we do."

We assumed that she was on track and about ready to put everything together. But as of two days ago, she had nothing to show us. Moreover, she was unable to respond to a few fundamental technical questions about networking. It was then that we realized that we were getting nowhere with this consultant. Is there any recourse to hiring an incompetent consultant?

A. If it's not too late, don't pay her. Otherwise, write the fee off as a contribution to experience and plan to be more involved with the next consultant's activities.

The next time you retain a consultant, make it clear that you expect results. If you are paying top dollar for experience and know-how, you should see some visible signs of progress each day. For example, a good consultant would have examined needs and prepared a draft microcomputer policy for your review by the end of the first week. Total billable time for such an activity should be between one and two days.

2.4.8.   Q. For the last 20 years I have been the director of increasingly larger DP shops. In my last position I was responsible for an annual budget of over $14 million. At 50, I have decided that 20 years is enough and will become an independent consultant specializing in matters relating to DP personnel, planning, and organization.

Do you have any guidelines that would help me price my services?

A. Consulting fees in the area of information services vary from $400 to $2,000, depending on the consultant's education, credentials, experience, and the proven ability to get the job done. There are a handful of information services consultants who demand fees of $3,000 to $10,000 per day.

In pricing your services, you must maintain a delicate balance between a fee that is acceptable and a fee that is high enough to demand respect. You could quote $1,000 per day and demand respect, but your credentials may not be convincing enough to land the job. It may take a little trial and error, but eventually your perceived worth and your actual worth will converge to a realistic fee.

Assuming that you have been a successful DP manager and can demonstrate your ability to get the job done, you might start at $500 per day. Add up to $200 per day extra if you feel your education and/or credentials are extraordinary. You can move up or down from there depending on the receptiveness of potential clients.

2.4.9.   Q. For the past five years I have had responsibility for the DP department (about 20 people). I'll be the first to admit that I have neglected it in favor of my primary responsibilities in accounting and finance.

Being in the public sector, we cannot keep up with DP salaries and, as a result, have lost most of our best people. With our current DP staff, our DP department is faltering.

Momentum is building to get out of the DP business and bring in a facilities management group. Such a group has proposed that they take over the entire DP operation. They said that they can move into our present facility and use their software to do everything we are doing now, and do it for less than we are currently spending. Is this possible?

A. Do *what* for less? It may be possible for the facilities management company to reduce DP costs and maintain the status quo over the short term, but is that what you want? You are apparently not satisfied with things the way they are.

Implied in the company's proposal is that services over and above the existing level of service will be billed. Don't overlook this important cost consideration.

External operation of the computer center has proved a smart decision for many organizations, but not for all. You never "get out of the DP business." Top management has an ongoing responsibility to relate information needs and priorities to the DP department. Whether run by an outside company or internally, it is top management's responsibility to provide strategic direction.

I detect from your letter that you expect to be absolved of further DP responsibilities once the facilities management company takes over. However, it doesn't work that way. If you continue to be aloof from DP, then don't expect any quantum leaps in the quality of the DP services.

2.4.10.   Q. A brochure caught the eye of our president, and he asked me to make the arrangements for the presentation of an in-house seminar. I contacted the DP management firm and requested a quote. A representative of the firm quoted $3,500, which I thought was a bit high for a half-day seminar. After voicing my concern, he asked what I thought was fair. We settled on $2,000, but I still thought the fee was high for a canned presentation.

The person assigned to present the seminar knew nothing about our environment and was embarrassingly ill prepared. He was unable to answer simple questions or elaborate on his own transparencies. What should have been a good seminar turned out to be a waste of time and reflected poorly on me.

The final blow came when the bill arrived with almost $1,000 of expenses tacked on to the quoted fee. Do we have any recourse?

A. It is unethical to attempt to price gouge an unsuspecting client. The consulting firm should have inquired about your environment and quoted you a fair price from the start.

Even though it is common practice to bill expenses over and above the fee, this should have been documented in writing or at least mentioned in your initial conversation.

Moreover, the consulting firm sent someone who was not qualified and as a result wasted the time of the people in attendance and caused embarrassment to you.

Unfortunately, your only economically feasible recourse is to appeal to the consulting firm's sense of responsibility. Make the firm's management aware of your dissatisfaction, both verbally and in writing.

If the firm is reputable and these practices are uncharacteristic, then I would anticipate that they will apologize and reimburse the expense portion of the bill—and perhaps the entire amount. But if your interaction with this firm was representative of how it does business, don't expect a reply.

2.4.11. Q. My company is upgrading its computer-aided design capabilities by installing the new generation of CAD equipment. Our in-house expertise is dated and we know that we need help in the selection, implementation, and application of the new hardware. We narrowed the field down to two consultants. One is a full-time CAD/CAM consultant and the other is an engineering professor doing consulting on the side.

The people involved with the project are impressed by the professor, but he is limited in the amount of time that he can devote to us. All of us agreed that he is just the person we need. On the other hand, the professional consultant is willing to make a "total commitment" to our project. We think that eventually he can do the job, but his credentials fall short of the professor's and he has an apparent lack of knowledge in certain areas.

My boss prefers the professional consultant because of his expressed "total commitment" and, possibly, because his fee is about $200 a day less than the professor's. Those who must work with the consultant, including myself, have recommended the professor. Have other companies been satisfied with their part-time professor consultants?

A. I would always opt for a little very good advice and guidance over lot of mediocre advice and guidance. Hire the professor—the tone of your letter implies that you would never be satisfied with the professional consultant. An effective client/consultant relationship demands that the clients have confidence in their consultant, whether the consultant is a career consultant, a professor, or someone "in between" jobs.

The best consultants take steps to ensure that the client is part of and benefits from the learning curve. The full-time consultant's "total commitment" indicates to me that the expertise garnered during this project may walk out the door when the consultant's contract is terminated.

part iii

Information Systems

3.1 INFORMATION SYSTEMS DEVELOPMENT AND IMPLEMENTATION

Methodologies, Standards, and Procedures

3.1.1. Q. A consultant recommended that the start of a few large new development projects be delayed by at least one year. This development slowdown is designed to free up MIS resources that can be allocated to documentation, reorganization, and the development of standards and procedures.

I report to a VP who supports the recommendations in theory but is reluctant to delay the development of what he considers to be essential systems. Even though everybody is in agreement with the recommendations, they are being ignored by top management. Any support?

A. During the growth of every information services department, there is a point in time at which the mess created to date must be "cleaned up." The consultant has identified that time as now.

Continued new systems development, in the absence of a rigorous development framework and standards, can only result in systems of marginal quality. Ask corporate managers if that is what they want. If management insists that the projects be continued, tell them that you will be happy to continue but cannot be responsible for the quality of the end product.

A well-ordered information systems department can produce more and better services. Over the long term, these "essential systems" will be insignificant when compared to the benefits derived from the proposed development slowdown.

3.1.2. Q. Could I suggest that you use "Turnaround Time" to investigate standards, procedures, and documentation? Would you ask your readers for their comments on the various commercial design or documentation methodologies: how well they work, how long they took to install and be used effectively, why they didn't work, and how they failed. Their comments would be valuable to the DP community.

A. I agree that this information would be valuable to the DP community and would like to invite readers to respond to one or all of your questions.

Author's note: Reader response was brisk to this request. Two insightful replies follow.

3.1.3.   Q. I am responding to your request in "Turnaround Time" for information relative to installation of commercial systems development methodologies.

All other things being equal, smaller DP organizations can and do implement faster than larger ones. DP organizations with 25 to 50 analysts and programmers typically get the methodology installed in 9 to 12 months. Very large DP organizations (over 200 analysts and programmers) may never get fully implemented according to my definition (as follows). Again, great benefits may be gained from the "journey" to install the methodology. The problem is, they just never get to the destination.

Installing a methodology is not a technical challenge; it is a social one. In reality, we are asking people to change the way they do things. These people (particularly analysts) tend to view themselves as implementers of change, rather than objects of it.

Organizations that treat the implementation of system development methodologies as a formal project have done so in shorter time and with higher success. This means having a project leader, a well defined and documented project plan, and regular and meaningful project reviews.

I do not believe you can say that implementation of a methodology is complete until all of the following have been accomplished:

- Management has issued and intends to enforce a set of policies which are consistent with the methodology.
- Management has budgeted for the administrative resources that are needed to support continued success of the methodology.
- User managers are setting the priorities for the project and DP is out of the "priority-setting business."
- Users are committed to the projects and accept their roles as project sponsors and quality reviewers.
- Pilot projects with regular quality review are well along in following the methodology and all new projects will be started under the methodology.
- The staff has been trained.

- The methodology has been customized to suit the local environment and a sufficient quantity of manuals and forms are available.
- The documentation turnover process to users, operations, and systems is functionally smooth.
- Updating of documentation on older but volatile systems is underway.
- Project team members are reporting their time utilization and their progress regularly.
- Regular project status reports are issued by project managers.

A. Performance measures should be established in order to evaluate the effectiveness of a project to implement a system development methodology. Your list of performance measures is well conceived and will surely be helpful to many DP managers who have implemented or are considering implementing a methodology.

Author's note: Another case history involving the implementation of a commercial systems development methodology follows.

3.1.4.   Q. In response to a "Turnaround Time" question concerning system design methodologies, I submit the following response.

We use a modified version of a popular commercial systems development methodology. We installed it four years ago and are only now seeing positive results.

Reluctance to using a structured design methodology was very strong and still remains fairly high because a structured approach does tend to take longer. Adapting to a structured design methodology has been more painful for our management people than for our system analysts because of the extended time required to produce the finished system project.

We are slowly beginning to realize that the benefits derived from implementing a system that had followed a structured design methodology far outweighed the time saved by using a "seat-of-the-pants" approach.

In our situation, implementing a methodology has been like breeding elephants . . .

- All work takes place on a high level.
- It is accomplished with a great deal of shouting and screaming.
- And it takes about two years to see the final results.

A. What more can I say?

3.1.5.   Q. Recently I was assigned the responsibility of compiling and maintaining a design methodology for our DP division. Since I have very little experience in this area, I was relying primarily on integrating and updating the existing documentation forms and procedures. We have many forms, a few written procedures and a rather extensive programming standards manual.

At one time or another, just about everybody in the division has contributed in some way to the existing standards and procedures. All of these people except one approve of the way I am compiling the design methodology. However, I disagree with the person who wrote the 75-page programming standards manual. He believes that there are enough good points that it should be included in the new design methodology manual.

Should programming standards be made a part of a design methodology manual?

A. I am assuming that your manual encompasses the systems development process and therefore programming. Contrary to popular belief, there is not a law that states that DP methodologies, standards, and policies should be compiled in the same volume. For every successful methodology I could show you ten reasonable methodologies that are not used, primarily because of the inclusion of unnecessary material.

As a rule of thumb—keep it simple. A common fault is to include tutorial material like how to design systems using structured approaches or programming standards. This complicates the methodology, making it more difficult to understand and use.

The programming standards should be placed in a separate manual.

Author's note: The next Q&A expands on this theme.

3.1.6.   Q. I have been reassigned from my project manager's position to a special projects group. My assignment is to compile a manual with guidelines for systems development and standards for programming. My only qualifications are that I am familiar with the life cycle and my boss says I am the only one who can write a coherent memo.

The decision has already been made to develop these guidelines in house. Any ideas about where to start?

A. You have been given two separate assignments. A systems development methodology and programming standards would normally be placed in separate manuals.

Organize the systems development methodology by the phases (typically four to seven) of the information systems life cycle, and identify and describe the activities to be accomplished for each phase. These activity descriptions include personnel involved and their responsibilities, criteria for decisions, considerations, approaches to a solution, and cross-references to other methodology activities. Ten to 20 of these activities should be designated as milestone activities for project management purposes.

The methodology should also contain forms, formats, guidelines, and instructions for all systems, programming, operations, and user documentation.

The programming standards manual should contain descriptions and illustrative uses of local programming conventions. Avoid tutorial text. This is a common problem. Tutorial material is not only unnecessary, but the added verbiage makes these manuals hard to use. Give your colleagues credit for their professionalism and knowledge. Your task is to create the framework for systems development and provide standards for program uniformity. Emphasize "what to do" not "how to do it."

3.1.7. Q. The 50 programmers and analysts where I work use 50 different approaches to design programs and systems. The basic objective is to get the job done and nobody cares how you do it.

My former employer did not use a specific design methodology, but management encouraged us to use Warnier diagrams and to follow the basic guidelines of structured programming. Although our approaches were not very sophisticated, the final result was far superior to anything here.

I have been here a month. Do you think I should suggest using the techniques that I used before?

A. You have a golden opportunity to be a hero, but don't blow it by coming on as a know-it-all after only one month on the job.

Since you are not required to follow any standard procedures or documentation practices, inform your immediate supervisor that you would like to use the approaches that proved effective in your previous job. Ask your supervisor to observe your work and provide feedback on the applicability of these techniques to the existing environment.

If your supervisor is favorably impressed, you might discuss the benefits derived from having all programmers and analysts use a few basic standard approaches and techniques. You may well be the catalyst for everything from improving system quality to raising morale.

3.1.8. Q. Three years ago I compiled a manual for system development. It also contains documentation standards. Since that time it has been used only sporadically, if at all. I am not in a position to demand

or even request that programmers and analysts follow these standards.

How do I get people to use the manual?

A. Many such manuals are used primarily to collect dust. It is unfortunate because these manuals are usually the result of substantial effort and,
if properly used, could improve system quality and department operations.
Without any specifics, I would assume that your problems parallel those in
similar circumstances: lack of management support, training, well-defined responsibilities, and manual quality.

Standards manuals, of any kind, must be sold from the top down. It is
a waste of time and money to distribute a system development manual without
management support. Your task now is to persuade information services management that their support of this manual is essential. The benefits, both intangible and tangible, are overwhelming.

Conduct periodic training sessions on the objectives of the methodology,
how to use the manual, and procedures for quality control. The mere distribution of a standards manual does not guarantee that people will use it.

A standards manual must be accompanied by procedures that define specific responsibilities. For example, the project leader might be assigned the
responsibility for the accurate completion of all new development and maintenance documentation.

Has it ever crossed your mind that the document you compiled is of
questionable quality? I've seen hundreds of information systems manuals.
Some are so poorly conceived and written that they are actually more trouble
than they are worth. In these cases I sympathize with those who refuse to use
them. Ask an unbiased and knowledgeable person for an opinion of the quality of your manual. A less-than-glowing evaluation should be followed up with
revisions or perhaps a rewrite.

3.1.9.   Q. I am a senior analyst in the computer services department
of a large company. We are responsible for providing services to all
departments within the company. I have been asked to initiate a review
of the procedures currently in place to develop cost estimates for the
design and implementation of new systems. Our current procedures
have not been yielding consistently accurate estimates. Can you recommend any procedures being used successfully elsewhere?

A. There are several prerequisites to making consistently accurate
cost estimates. A system development methodology is necessary to provide the
framework (phases, activities and milestones) for estimation and the collection
of historical data. To minimize in-progress revisions and therefore variations
in estimation, the feasibility study should include a preliminary general sys-

tems design that provides sufficient detail to define the project's scope. Estimation is still very much an art and not a science; the wisdom of experienced personnel is a must.

Author's note: The delphi technique, a procedure for determining consensus estimates, is discussed in Part 1, Section 1.2, Planning.

3.1.10. **Q.** In four months, we are scheduled to implement a home-grown manufacturing resource planning system (MRP). I am the project leader. While drawing up the conversion plan, it became apparent that we had a real problem. The new MRP system is such a radical change from the way we have traditionally handled manufacturing systems that the conversion calls for some structural reorganization and some facilities changes.

The differences in approach and the scattering of personnel make parallel conversion impossible with current resources. We considered hiring ten temporary people for two months, but that proposal fell through when the managers involved decided it was a waste of time and money to train temporary people on the old procedures.

Although I have recommended a direct conversion, the users say this is out of the question. They offer no alternative. Do you have one?

A. With the implementation of more and more integrated on-line information systems, direct conversion has become an increasingly appealing alternative to the traditional parallel conversion. The implementation of an MRP system is an invitation to go "cold turkey" with direct conversion. A phased conversion is not as applicable to MRP as it is to other systems.

Offset the greater risk of direct conversion with extra-thorough system testing and user training. I would suggest that you continue to press for a direct conversion effort.

3.1.11. **Q.** We are working closely with an established software vendor to implement a package that has been successfully implemented in 20 similar institutions. Since certain internal procedures must remain intact, we have contracted the vendor to modify the package to meet our requirements.

In this joint venture we have met every milestone and the vendor has not, but our technical people assure me that if everything goes right, the system will be up on time. We must be ready by a certain date or wait another year.

Our initial schedule allotted 12 weeks for data conversion and parallel operation. Missed milestones have reduced that to six. Twelve was tight, and six may be impossible. Our advisory committee has mandated the software changes and is measuring our progress against those institutions that installed the package as is. The advisory committee is aware of the delays but thinks we should implement no matter what. How can we convince them that we are in serious trouble?

A. You are unnecessarily courting a confrontation with disaster. I would suggest that you convene those interested and affected persons and identify intermediate milestones at one-week intervals. Based on information available, a go/no-go decision should be made at each milestone. In your situation, a doomed project pressed to an untimely completion is a waste of valuable resources.

Documentation

3.1.12.   Q. My company has recently formed a standards and documentation group. I am the manager of this small group which has two others besides myself. The duties of the group are still not well defined, but a more immediate problem has surfaced.

The group was formed because documentation was so lax. Since the very first day, programmers have been giving us source code listings without accompanying documentation and asking us to complete the documentation. This has become an impossible task and a point of contention in that I believe such documentation is the programmer's responsibility. Am I correct?

A. Your most immediate task should be to work with DP management to define the duties and responsibilities of your newly formed group. The following list of possible duties and responsibilities may be helpful to your initial analysis:

- Develop and maintain the systems development methodology.
- Control a library of existing applications documentation.
- Insure compliance with the methodology.
- Perform quality assurance for documentation.
- Serve as procedures and standards advisors to users and DP personnel.
- Conduct training in use of the methodology and preparation of the documentation.
- Develop and maintain programming standards.
- Develop and maintain design standards and approaches.
- Maintain historical statistics on dollar, manpower, and time utilization.

- Generate management reports.
- Gather feedback on methodology and update as appropriate.

Note that the actual documentation process was not included in the given list. The programmer is responsible for compilation of the complete program documentation package according to the instructions set forth in the design methodology. Documentation is not something you do after system implementation. Documentation, if done correctly, is an aid to program development and is therefore part of the program development process. The same is true of system documentation.

Asking anyone, other than the program author, to document a program from the source listing is an unnecessary waste of manpower.

3.1.13. Q. My boss consistently commits the department to deadlines which are nearly impossible to meet. The result is a mediocre job performed in a crisis atmosphere. Furthermore, the lack of documentation makes maintenance a nightmare! What can be done?

A. The resultant system notwithstanding, your boss is making three critical errors (among others). First, the product of his overcommitment is a system that is probably less than the user wants. Second, people must be able to take pride in their work in order to realize any kind of job satisfaction. Your boss has denied you this opportunity. Third, no system is truly implemented until the documentation is completed.

I assume your boss is meeting the deadlines, but is it worth it? The cost of systems development and implementation is but a small percentage of the total cost over the life of the system. Hastily developed systems inevitably result in high maintenance cost. The best investment a company can make is to put enough money and time into a computer systems project to do it right the first time.

It is probably too much to ask that your boss recognize the shortcomings of his approach to systems development. After all, he is meeting his commitments. However, sooner or later your boss and the company must "pay the piper". I only hope that your boss reevaluates his approach before you and your colleagues are totally committed to systems maintenance and nobody is available for new systems development. If he doesn't, your boss may have no resources to commit.

3.1.14. Q. It is apparent that you are a staunch advocate of comprehensive documentation. Is there such a thing as overkill? Under the guise of documentation, one of the other managers writes memos to everybody on any subject. In my opinion, many (perhaps even all) are totally unnecessary and a waste of everyone's time. Surely you can't defend this mode of documentation.

A. You're right, I can't. Unfortunately, some people are just "memo writers." To these people, even the most meaningless happenstance merits a memo. These memos are not documentation.

Memos do have their place. Well-written memos that document findings or status are always appropriate. For example, the chairman of the MIS steering committee should send a formal memo to users who have submitted a major request for MIS service. These memos might reflect the committee's decision and provide supporting statements for both the users information and a permanent record. As another example, some internal procedures require a memo from project leaders when a project falls behind schedule or is expected to fall behind schedule. Such a memo might contain an overview of project progress, a description of extraordinary problems that have caused or are expected to cause delays in progress, and an approach to solutions to the problems. These and other memos which reflect findings and status have immediate and historic value and can be considered DP documentation.

Like so many others, your friend appears to be addicted to memo writing and must have a daily fix. I am not sure that there is a cure. Be leery when documentation is used as justification for obviously unnecessary memorandums.

3.1.15.   Q. I enjoy reading "Turnaround Time." My question is: Are there standards for the number of pages of documentation which should be developed for each 10,000 lines of code (pages/10,000 LOC) for general business systems applications written in COBOL or BASIC? By documentation, I mean the total system documentation, including the operator's and user's manuals.

A. No, nor should such a standard exist. Standards are a necessary ingredient to successful DP operation, but too many standards can impede creativity and productivity. Pages/10,000 LOC is a perfect example of a standard that is not only unnecessary but counterproductive.

Too many variables exist in a given system to base the volume of documentation on pages/10,000 LOC. System complexity, extent of user involvement, on line or batch, and many other variables would combine to make this standard unmanageable.

3.1.16.   Q. I am director of MIS for a relatively small but very involved DP shop. We have been successful in implementing new, cost-justified, well-designed applications.

My systems and programming staff is young, aggressive, and

very talented. We seem to always cover every aspect of application development (including timely delivery) with the exception of user documentation. This never seems to get done. Months later we are still called upon to rectify problems that should have been answered through documentation.

My staff readily admits the need is urgent. I have tried extra days off, bonuses, and job elimination in hopes of changing this around. Do you have any suggestions for this "too busy for documentation" problem?

A. If you have time to continually rectify problems resulting from poorly written user manuals, you have time to do it right the first time. Your problems may be founded more on lack of know-how than willingness.

In theory, the contents of the user documentation is embedded in the system and programming documentation. The task is to transcribe and reformat appropriate documentation such that it can be understood and not misinterpreted by the user.

Establish a standard format for user manuals and for follow-up user training. The following user manual format has been used successfully: objectives of system; description of system; work flow and general operating procedures; instructions for completing and understanding input/output; data collection and update procedures; control; and a glossary of unique terms. A user training program should include: system purpose and objectives; differences between old and new procedures; overview of system operation; use of the user manual; and duties and responsibilities of all concerned.

Have you considered hiring a technical writer or documentalist to assist in the production of user manuals?

3.1.17. Q. We don't have a single system with up-to-date documentation. Good documentation was a top priority with my former employer, but it is all but neglected with my current employer. My team devotes much of its time to trying to learn what was done in the past and what changes have been made.

Documentation does not seem to be an issue with DP or user managers. How can I and several others that are concerned convince management that we are digging our own graves?

A. I've said it before but I'll say it again: *Documentation is part of the system development and maintenance process.* It's not something you do hurriedly at the end of the project. When done properly, documentation is an excellent development tool, and over the long term, a sound financial investment.

I would expect that your managers have adopted a short-term outlook

forsaking system quality and ease of maintenance for an expedient implementation. This "fly now, pay later" attitude towards documentation is very expensive and basically indefensible. You might suggest that a staff meeting be
devoted to discussing the merits of documentation and what should be done
about it. Management should get the message.

3.1.18.   Q. I have been assigned the unenviable task of documenting
many programs which have never before been documented and have
been repeatedly patched and modified. The systems in question have
no user manuals and the original authors are no longer working here.
    How would you suggest that I approach this difficult task of
documenting programs after the fact?

A. I am not convinced that you should be documenting these particular programs at all. Documenting old programs can be enormously time
consuming, not to mention frustrating. I would suggest that you at least address the possibility of starting from scratch; it may be less expensive in the
long run. Programs that were developed and are subsequently maintained
without documentation are usually poorly designed to begin with. It is unlikely
that a good documentation package will help these costly maintenance night-
mares.

If you feel that you must proceed, you and your boss need to ask your-
selves a question: "What is the expected life of the systems involved?" As a
rule of thumb, document undocumented systems if the system is expected to
remain operational for at least two more years. If you anticipate repairing
these systems within two years, make the best of what you have.

If the decision is to document, do not be as rigorous as you would for a
new program. Extract critical documentation items from your existing methodology, then follow the same pattern for each program.

*Author's note: In the next Q&A a reader offers some good advice to this
correspondent.*

3.1.19.   Q. I would like to add some specifics to your response to a
person who was doomed to documenting dinosaurs. We follow these
guidelines in updating the documentation of old systems and programs which have no documentation or poor documentation.

1. Documenting the data flow is more important than documenting the programs.
2. Set a time limit for documenting a system.
3. Begin with the identification of all programs (not program internals).

4. Compile data flow diagrams showing all I/O for each program (files, datasets, reports, and screens).

5. Now, if time permits, identify the worst programs and list the programming tricks that they use.

We have found that this much documentation of "old" programs goes a long way.

A. Your guidelines are good, but allow yourself enough flexibility to spend more time on the redocumentation of old systems that are extremely volatile and critical to organizational operation (and sometimes survival). Give these dynamic systems more attention than the relatively stable systems that have cumbersome, but acceptable, documentation.

3.1.20.   Q. Until a few months ago, I worked for five years in a dead-end position editing technical manuals. Recently, I transferred to a more challenging position with a newly formed documentation group in the MIS department. The job is definitely challenging, but nobody told me about the frustration.

There are three of us in the group and none of us has a computer background. Our jobs, as they were described to us, would entail the writing of user systems manuals and, perhaps somewhere down the road, some user education. We were to take the system write-ups provided to us by programmers and analysts, and write "user-friendly" manuals.

The three of us are part of the systems and programming section, and everybody seems to think that our function is to document their programs, as well as write the user systems manuals.

Programmers literally dump program listings on us. They ask us to prepare flowcharts and document program listings. When we approached our boss and told him that we do not feel qualified to do this kind of documentation, he told us to learn.

Do documentation specialists in other companies document programs?

A. Documentalists involved in program documentation would normally clean up completed but rough documentation that is provided by programmers. It is extremely inefficient to ask someone not involved with designing the logic and writing the code of a program to document it. First of all, documentation is a by-product of the development process, not something that is done hurriedly after a program is running. Second, the original programmer is in a much better position to produce documentation than you.

Documentation is viewed by many as an unpleasant task that is either done haphazardly or, if possible, avoided. To these people, the establishment of your group meant no more documentation.

A well-written program is usually accompanied by good, but not necessarily clean, documentation. If your job description continues to include program documentation, then it should be limited to a clean-up operation.

Programmers should be given minimum documentation standards that must be met before programs are submitted to you for final documentation.

Quality Assurance

3.1.21.   Q. I have recently been hired by a well-known company in the technical data processing area. The company management has decided to create a quality assurance group with the emphasis on protecting their on-line production systems from undue downtime, either from program or other software error. My managers do not seem to be able to give us a clear-cut direction on how to do this and have asked the newly formed quality assurance organization to present their views on how to perform this function. We have come up with numerous proposals but keep running into walls. Any advice you have will be welcome.

A. Studies have shown that it takes approximately 50 times the effort to rectify errors found after implementation than for those found during the design phase. The message is loud and clear! The quality assurance group should be an integral part of the development effort from the time the project is approved, not just after implementation.

The quality assurance function, though well established in some organizations, is nonexistent in most. Properly charged, the Q.A. group can have a positive effect on the quality of design, documentation, and ultimately, the efficiency and effectiveness of the system. Quality assurance encourages the do-it-right-the-first-time approach. A good many computer centers are tiring of having to do systems over and have opted to establish a Q.A. group and integrate it into the development process.

3.1.22.   Q. I just celebrated my tenth year in data processing. I have worked my tail off and have spent many sleepless weekends at the computer center. Yet, neither I nor my product (software) is well thought of in other areas of our business.

Software quality is attributed directly to me and my colleagues.

Users deserve some credit for the level of quality. When we estimate that it will take two people one year to complete a project, they ask the same two people to do it in six months. Halfway through the project one person (half of the team) is reassigned to another "priority" project. Just before scheduled implementation, a major system modification is requested.

What can I look forward to in my second decade? Is there a light at the end of the tunnel?

A. You have made an excellent point. For any given project a change in quality, scope, resources, or schedule will inevitably invoke a change in one or several of the others.

As you indicate, quality is usually forsaken for changes in schedule, resources, and scope. There is no reason why those involved cannot be made aware of the impact of their decisions.

User awareness may be the light at the end of the tunnel.

3.1.23. Q. Although the division director set it at 50 percent, a more realistic assessment of our maintenance effort is 80 percent and growing. I would say that half the service requests that we receive are not worth a tenth of the effort that we put forth to respond.

Any ideas on how we can better control these requests?

A. Is there an effective standardized procedure for submitting service requests? Is the end user responsible for completing the service request? Do you have a chargeback system that realistically reflects the cost of the service? Are project prioritization criteria documented and followed? Are requests for service assigned a priority with respect to corporate objectives?

Is quality emphasized during systems developments? Do you periodically review existing systems to proactively identify system inefficiencies and needs? Does MIS management know how many resources are devoted to maintenance? Are users aware of the impact of their requests?

You should have responded "yes" to each of the above questions. A company's commitment to the maintenance effort is directly proportional to the number of "no" answers. The obvious solution is to do whatever it takes to make sure you answer "yes" to as many of these questions as possible.

3.2 DATA MANAGEMENT

3.2.1. Q. We are in the process of evaluating data base management systems and expect to begin the conversion process within the year. As an IBM user, we have a variety of options and generally understand the trade-offs. I would appreciate any insights you might have regarding recent breakthroughs or current research that might affect our decision.

A. Existing commercially available data base management systems are passive and respond only when queried. Current research on "alerter" systems promises to enhance the functional capabilities of information systems by enabling the user to assume a dynamic attitude toward the data base. Briefly stated, an alerter system monitors a data base and takes predefined actions when it detects the occurrence of a dynamically specified condition. Alerter systems will add a new dimension to current commercially available data bases and, therefore, to the computer-assisted decision-making process.

I would anticipate that alerters will soon be a commercial reality. Initial alerters will be dependent on a specific DBMS; therefore, you might ask potential vendors about their plans for incorporating alerter capabilities.

3.2.2. Q. One of our vice-presidents recently returned from a week-long seminar and asked if we had a decision support system. I asked him if he could be more specific and he said that he could not. Apparently the seminar leaders told a group of executives that a decision support system would essentially provide them with up-to-the-minute information in any format at any time. We're good, but we're not that good.

I believe that some executive seminars do more harm than good. They give the people in attendance unrealistic impressions of the capabilities of a typical computer center. Do you agree?

A. I agree that the much-ballyhooed term *decision support systems* is routinely abused. People who write and talk about decision support systems tend to imply that all one has to do to ascend to information heaven is to install a decision support system (DSS). Of course, the implementers know that it's not that simple. It's much easier to put the burden of explanation (and implementation) on an MIS department.

DSS is another one of these terms, like *minicomputer*, that means different things to different people. In conversational computerese, communication is much more efficient when people just say what they mean. The typical end user would be better served if we referenced specific decision support tools: fourth generation (query) languages, electronic spreadsheets, business graphics, linear programming models, expert systems, and so on.

3.2.3. Q. I often read about "totally integrated" companies. Our organization is far from integrated, even though we have relied on database software for almost a decade. Where are these "totally integrated" companies?

A. I am unable to confirm that they exist. Certainly the management of any MIS department would aspire to integrating as much of the corporate data base and information flow as possible. It has been my experience that truly state-of-the-art companies will fall well short of total integration. We have the technology to realize total integration, but in practice, political exigencies, lack of funding, and more immediate demands preclude the utopian MIS, at least for the time being.

3.2.4.   Q. Should the word "data" be treated as singular or plural? I see both "data is" and "data are."

A. There are two schools of thought on this. Some publishers prefer to treat data as a collective singular, others prefer the traditional grammatical usage. To me, however, "data is" still has the ring of "they is."

3.3 SECURITY

3.3.1.   Q. A few years ago, I took over our family-owned savings and loan business. I managed our computer center for five years during the 1970s and only recently have I become aware of how vulnerable we are to computer crime. Are there any signals that might foretell the possibility of a computer crime?

A. Computer crimes occur methodically over a long period of time. Any physical or behavioral change may be so gradual that it may go undetected. The best way to thwart computer crime is to take precautionary measures. Do this by conducting a very thorough risk assessment each year.

I encourage both MIS and user managers to get more involved technically in the work of their subordinates. Ask detailed questions of subordinates, even if you do not fully understand the answers. The rationale behind this type of questioning is that subordinates are given the impression that management is right on top of what they are doing. This perception may be just enough to dispel any thoughts of "fast money."

3.3.2.   Q. My employer, a bank, is considering the installation of data encryption equipment and has asked me for information regarding its usage and effectiveness in industry. I have been unable to find any articles, statistics, or case studies to contribute to the evaluation. I would appreciate any help.

A. In the scheme of things, cryptography has been surprisingly insignificant; therefore, usage statistics are scarce. However, the day is coming when encryption/decryption hardware and software will be standard on all workstations.

At present, we have a chicken and egg situation. Companies do not feel they need data encryption/decryption, and vendors are not going to make it available at a reasonable price until they do. Potential users, such as banks, are still reluctant to foot the expense of field installation of encryption/decryption capabilities.

The equivalent of over one trillion dollars is electronically transferred via data communications each day. That's a lot of vulnerability. Shortly after the first truly catastrophic financial disaster, bankers will demand cryptography and vendors will supply it at reasonable cost, but probably not before then.

3.3.3.   **Q.** At lunch the conversation between myself, two other applications programmers, and a systems programmer revolved around the ease with which any one of us could embezzle tens of thousands of dollars from our employer (a bank), and get away with it. We talked of several well-documented electronic scams that would work here.

Surprisingly, each of us was able to suggest ways to pilfer funds from the bank. Most involved simple program modification, but the systems programmer's scheme was more exotic. He suggested ways to intercept and modify certain data transmissions.

This candid conversation made us very sensitive to how vulnerable we are to computer crime. My co-workers agree that something must be done, but top management continues to place a very low priority on implementing security measures. How can we convince them of the potential for disaster and the importance of security safeguards?

A. A bank that downplays the threat of fraud is essentially playing hockey without a goalie. A hockey coach may reallocate his resources for a short-term gain, but in so doing, he makes his team vulnerable to the quick score.

The move to more and more electronic funds transfer has a multiplier effect on system vulnerability. I am continually amazed that high-level bankers are content to concern themselves with traditional banking matters and defer decisions on data security until something happens.

They must be told emphatically that a computer heist can do much more than clean out the teller drawers! Perhaps you and your colleagues can bring this point home by discussing, and even demonstrating, how vulnerable your bank is to an electronic heist.

Security is implemented in degrees. No organization can be totally secure, but the technology is available to substantially decrease the opportunity for computer crime. I hope your warnings are heeded.

3.3.4. Q. I am writing to you in hopes of obtaining information on security and control for computer-based systems.

Specifically, I am interested in information on data base and file security, disaster planning and recovery, preventing access to computer sites, as well as securing the entire system.

Additionally, any information you may have on safeguarding the system to prevent unauthorized use and/or articles on restart procedures should a computer system be sabotaged would be appreciated.

A. You've asked for the Watergate tapes, the history of the United States (1940–present) and the court records of the IBM antitrust suit. Most industry journals publish regularly on the topics you listed.

Ask your corporate reference librarian, or one from a local university, to help you identify appropriate articles, papers, and books on specific topics of interest.

Even with the untold number of pages written on security and controls, the industry is either not reading or not believing what they read. I regularly see flagrant violations of security maxims and/or systems with limited or nonexistent controls. Some companies and public agencies are living on borrowed time. Annual system audits and risk analyses to evaluate the adequacy of controls and security should be routine procedures. The breadth of your question leads me to believe that you have been assigned these tasks.

3.4 LEGAL IMPLICATIONS AND ETHICS

3.4.1. Q. Our company purchased some software recently for which one of the company's officers had to sign a single-CPU usage licensing agreement. Our company also contracted out work to a consultant. Knowing ahead of time that the consultant would need to use the purchased software on his system in order to complete the work, I notified my superior (an officer of the company) that there was a conflict between the license agreement and allowing the consultant to use the purchased software on his system. I informed my superior that this conflict would have to be addressed and resolved before it was to take place.

When the consultant arrived to discuss matters as well as obtain a copy of the purchased software, I was told by my superior to copy the software. I refused since the conflict had not been resolved. My superior then informed me to tell another to do the copying, which I did, for I was not prepared to fight my last stand at that moment. My superior justified the copying because (1) the consultant would only use it for a short time, (2) there was a physical distance between our company and the consultant's place of work that prevented him from coming in on a daily basis, and (3) if the consultant did come in, then there was no way that we could reasonably prevent him from copying it anyway. I did not consider any of these reasons valid, for I felt it was a question of professional ethics.

Some time has passed now, but I will not forget this incident. I still do not feel comfortable about what happened. Should I have made an issue out of it? Should I have taken more (or less) action than I did? Should I still "blow the whistle" and inform the vendor that my company illegally copied their software?

A. The breach of a legally binding agreement cannot be condoned, but it is water under the bridge now. A more appropriate action would have been to explain the situation to the vendor and ask permission for the consultant to use the proprietary software on his system. Given that the consultant would agree to using the software on contract-related work only, the vendor would probably approve such a request. By granting permission, they gain your goodwill and an opportunity to gain another customer.

The appropriate procedure would have been for the consultant to write a letter confirming his limited-use intent. After receiving a satisfactory letter, the vendor would then follow up with an approval letter to both your company and the vendor.

If the vendor refused, your company should have asked the consultant to make arrangements necessary to complete the work within the framework of the licensing agreement.

Author's note: More than one reader disagreed with my soft-glove treatment of this issue. Read on.

3.4.2. Q. While I appreciate your suggestions to an employee regarding the unauthorized copying of software, I am disappointed with your comment that it is now "water under the bridge." This type of attitude has allowed so much water to go by that a raging sea has been growing at the doorsteps of many software houses. And many of these vendors are often equipped with less than a bucket to clean up the flood.

That one copy of software, now in unauthorized possession of a consultant, could easily spread like wild fire into the hands of other consultants and, eventually, to needing, and unsuspecting end-users. The horror stories that float their way back to the vendors are, indeed, horrible. Not only have the vendors lost control of their software (not to mention the revenues honestly due them), but the end-users often find themselves faced with law suits, losses and nonfunctioning computer systems that seem to go hand-in-hand with the unethical business practices of the software pirate.

The entire subject of software protection is demanding far more attention than the media have given it. Hoping for legislative protection and assistance fails to address the problems vendors are faced with, and it is costing time in which bootleggers could conceivably cripple the industry. The "spilled milk" attitude fails to realistically address the situation, a fact which often escapes those who are not trying to mop up the flood.

The situation has reached such proportions that some vendors, including my own company, have sought one another out in hopes of at least building a raft of common support among ourselves. The Association of Software Protection (ASP), though still primitive, is nevertheless an attempt to develop a unified defense. Had I responded to the question presented to you, I would have demanded he "blow the whistle" and let the vendor know what had occurred. And, just for the record, I hope the vendor isn't us.

A. I responded to the previous inquiry with the individual and circumstances in mind, and not with respect to the broader issue—abuse of proprietary software. I would like to initial your statements and provide a few of my own.

Software thievery is a crime, a severe crime that could have a devastating effect on the future of the software industry. The problem is compounded because existing circumstances make this piracy a low-risk crime committed by people with an amazing affinity for rationalization. A breach of contract is unlawful and there is no justification.

I have no immediate answers but I can use this space to appeal to the MIS professional's pride and sense of ethics to do what is right and just.

3.4.3. **Q.** I am 57 and puzzled. Two years ago I took early retirement after 24 years in computers and started working on a desktop computer in my bedroom. I enjoy the work and have produced two complete application packages. From time to time, to test the water, I write to advertising companies for jobs. I invariably tell them I am 57. No one ever bothers even to ask me for an interview, even though I occasionally offer my services on any basis whatsoever, not needing company benefits any more. The wording of the replies I receive, if I receive them, manifests a clumsy and pathetic attempt to appear not to discriminate on the basis of age. However, we all know, in this country age is considered a curse.

By contrast, two foreign employers on different continents have shown interest in me, even though I do not master the languages of their respective countries. As it happens, I don't need the jobs but merely want to know whether I am still lovable. I have concluded that the USA is too hung up in its concern with cosmetics or social security taxes or whatnot to qualify as a smart buyer of experienced technical labor. One more mark for the Japanese.

A. Not many people can boast 24 years of DP experience. Under the right circumstances, managers of short-handed information services departments would actively solicit your services. Unfortunately, the paradox of government intervention surfaces its ugly head—again.

Upon receipt of your resume, the information systems managers' rationale for their response might go something like this: "This man's resume is very impressive and he would certainly be an asset to our organization. His financial security is already taken care of and he is willing to take a lesser position for the sheer love of the information processing business. He's even willing to take a drastic cut in salary, status and work for no benefits. Employing him would be a mutually beneficial arrangement, but can we risk the possibility of age discrimination accusations? The next thing you know the federal government would be all over us. I suppose we have no option but to send him letter X2-1" (a letter similar to those you have received).

I do not see the situation reversing in the near future. Although I'm reluctant to say it, your best bet would be to approach potential employers as a private contractor desiring short-term work. I would like to invite employers to take advantage of this opportunity to hire these experienced professionals who do not necessarily need the work, but want to work.

3.4.4. Q. Regulation Y of the Federal Banking Regulations is supposed to limit computer activities of banks and bank holding companies to "services closely related to banking."

I work for a bank-owned service bureau and we do a variety of work for many customers. Applications include: accounts receivable, inventory control, address labeling, voter registration, local tax accounting, job costing, and many more, none of which could be considered closely related to banking.

Are we within the limits of Regulation Y? If not, how long do you think the banking examiners will allow us to continue doing these kinds of jobs?

A. Regulation Y is concerned with allowable nonbanking activities. The regulation limits data processing services to "financial, banking, and economic data;" however, the banking industry has adopted a rather broad interpretation.

You might have a little trouble with address labeling and voter registration, but with a little imagination you could make a case that all of your applications are within the limitations of Regulation Y.

Hundreds of other bank-owned service bureaus have interpreted Regulation Y in a similar manner. Since this interpretation is widely accepted, I would be surprised if you and the others were not permitted to continue the present mode of operation indefinitely.

3.4.5. Q. We market an on-line system for processing health claims (e.g., medical, dental, disability) and are constantly making revisions. Because of the revisions, we feel it necessary to define the difference between enhancements and a new system in our standard contract. Enhancements are included with the standard maintenance agreement, but a new system involves renegotiation.

Most of our clients are not DP oriented so they tend to feel that any change falls under the category of enhancements and is part of the service. We do not want to give away items which we feel warrant a separate charge and, in many cases, involve an expensive file conversion.

Can you suggest any definitions or explanation which may help us?

A. The difference is best explained in the context of the four stages of the system life cycle: birth, development, production, and death. Systems are dynamic and require *enhancements* during the production stage so they can continue to serve the DP and information needs of the company. The accumulation of system modifications eventually takes its toll and the information system becomes so cumbersome that it is no longer operationally or economically effective. It dies (last stage) and is reborn (first stage) as a *new system*.

An enhancement is integrated within the framework of an existing system. The design of a new system is in no way constrained by the design of the old system. A new system involves a fresh look at system requirements. It would normally result in a new data base design, I/O, and procedures.

If you develop a functionally adjacent module that is not within the scope of the original system, it is neither an enhancement or a new system. As such, it is a charge item and can be sold separately.

3.4.6. Q. I am in the auto parts business. About three years ago I considered purchasing a computer system for my business, but just could not justify spending so much money. So I bought a personal computer and several books, learned how to program, and designed my own program.

As I was learning, I was also thinking of a program for my stores, one that would be unique. Until now, the only programs available for my business were inventory systems with accounts receivable, accounts payable, and general ledger.

I developed a program to include cataloging (not available before) plus an accounting package, an inventory system, and automatic purchasing. You would answer the questions that came up on the screen, and the system would give you the part numbers: no more catalogs.

I had little programming knowledge, so I found a programmer with much more knowledge. We made an agreement. I would pay him and, if it worked out, we would start a company and split the stock. I was to put up the money and insight into the automotive business. He was to do the programming.

Since the project cost more than anticipated, my partner gave me 7 percent of his stock and I put in additional funds. I now hold 57 percent and he holds 43 percent of the stock.

When the program was about 75 percent complete, we unveiled our product at an automotive show. The program was the talk of the industry. We were approached by a competitive computer company that wanted an exclusive to our program and data base. Unbeknownst to me while I was negotiating with this company on behalf of our company, my partner was also talking with them.

The end result was that my partner removed all the equipment from our office, including the source program, data base, and all working terminals.

A week later I got a call from this competitive company telling me that they took a stock option on my partner's shares and gave him a work option. They sent me a copy of a proxy to vote, but refused to give me a copy of the contract which includes the work option. They insist that they have no trade secrets. After this, my partner returned the equipment.

This company still wants to make a deal. They want to purchase my shares, but at nowhere near the price of the exclusive deal we were negotiating before this all occurred.

After over two years of hard work, I am frustrated that a large corporation can come in and just take over. The computer laws seem vague and I know that a precedence is being set in this field.

Is there any advice that you could give me, especially regarding the laws and ethics in the computer field?

A. The laws protecting proprietary software provide some guidance for resolving legal disputes for common situations, but yours is not a common situation. However, the scope of your dilemma is surprisingly typical of cases that will be peppering our judicial system in the near future.

If your description of the course of events is accurate, I would have to assess your partner's actions as unethical. But illegal? That's another question.

Your partner could say that he was operating on the behalf of your company and, of course, he has the right to sell his stock in the company.

As for your desire to see the work option contract of your partner, I am not optimistic about a competitive company volunteering such information. You may, however, be able to get it through the courts.

Your auto parts software has a fair market price that is probably between the starting point for your initial negotiations and the company's most recent offer. As I see it, the final gun hasn't sounded. You still have some negotiating power.

A large software company will not market your product or anything similar, given the circumstances described in your letter. To do so would leave them vulnerable to unfavorable litigation against them.

I am hopeful that this unfortunate sequence of events can be resolved to the mutual benefit of you and the competing software company.

3.4.7. Q. I know for a fact that personal computers in my department have been used for the unauthorized duplication of proprietary software. Recently, I made it clear that I did not condone this type of activity. However, I learned through the grapevine that since that meeting, one package has been copied for home use.

Have other companies been successful in stopping software piracy? If so, what are they doing?

A. Every time I begin to think that the software pirates are losing the war, I am in some way reminded that the pilferage continues. Only recently, I listened as the president of a company (perhaps $30 million in sales) encouraged over 100 conference attendees to save money by copying proprietary software. Software vendors are very serious about eradicating this erosion of profits.

Any company that does not have a written policy regarding the duplication of proprietary software should draft one as soon as possible. For the purposes of individual protection, any manager responsible for microcomputers should distribute a memo that articulates the company's policy on the reproduction of proprietary software.

As further protection for the company and as a warning to users, many companies are producing stick-on labels that read something like this: Unauthorized duplication of copyright software is prohibited on this machine.

3.4.8. Q. While I have some sympathy for the difficulties encountered by personal computer software vendors protecting their proprietary interest, their stipulations on copying are impractical in a corporate environment. The current public relations campaign to get the public to conform to licensing protocols leads me to wonder whether our current practices are ethical.

We would never knowingly cheat or defraud anyone. However, our own procedures for distributing personal computer software within our own organization do not conform to the many and varied forms of words that software vendors wrap around their licenses.

We buy licenses for every PC that runs licensed software, but we try to avoid buying licenses when we just want to evaluate a package. Borrowed software is returned following evaluation and back-up copies are destroyed.

We issue copies, not the original software, to our production users, and we will not license anything we cannot copy. We do not reregister licensed software if it is moved to a different host PC or when we swap the original PC out for repair or upgrade.

These practices clearly do not conform to the requirements of many of the software licenses. Even though our practices are not intrinsically illegal, they could be regarded as being in breach of contract. However, we do not consider that we have damaged the interests of the vendors, and so any breach would be merely technical and have no financial value.

Our procedures are based on commercial pragmatism. Because of this, we do sign licenses that we do not intend to adhere to fully. Is this ethical?

A. A breach of contract, no matter how seemingly insignificant the infraction, is unlawful and, therefore, it is unethical.

It is common knowledge that people in business, government, and education have abused PC software license agreements, sometimes blatantly. People have openly recounted their abuses to me with a sense of pride of accomplishment. In reprisal for these abuses, some software vendors may have overreacted, in my opinion, in the stipulations and restrictions they set forth in their license agreement. Most companies simply use common sense in their treatment of a vendor's copyright.

A vendor-sponsored campaign to curb abuses is needed, but, I agree with you that we need a more pragmatic approach to the licensing of proprietary software. I would encourage the PC software industry to cooperate in developing a universal license agreement that is guided by common sense and fairness, and can be understood by all and enforced by the industry. As it is, a great many users are feeling pretty unethical about now.

3.4.9.   Q. My partner and I have a small computer systems consulting firm. The two of us and two part-timers can do just about anything that involves the use of personal computers or small minicomputers. Two years ago business was booming but today we are struggling. Until recently, clients were lined up at our door. Now, I am making cold calls to promote business.

We prepared a brochure which details our services and lists some of our previous clients. I received a call from a previous and current client who was irritated because we listed his company in our brochure without written permission. He asked that we remove his company's name from our brochure. We want to retain this company as a client, so we reprinted the brochure. We asked for and received permission to list the names of our other clients in the reprint. My question is, should we be listing clients in our brochure?

A. Omit the client list in favor of a carefully worded sentence that makes the point that you are well established in the area. Follow that sentence with a statement that expresses a willingness to provide references if so requested. Of course, you will need to compile a list of cooperative clients in the case that a prospective client follows up on your invitation.

The impression that I get when reading a brochure or ad piece that includes the names of clients is somewhere between flat and negative. It is not who you worked for that counts, it's what you did.

part iv

Education

4.1 ACADEMIC PROGRAMS

4.1.1.   Q. Perhaps you could distinguish between a college curriculum in management information systems and one in computer science. Why are there so few MIS programs and so many computer science programs?

A. Your question is substantive and has caused considerable confusion and discontent among employers, students, and university administrators and faculty.

The curricula are similar in that they both use the computer as a tool and deal with system design and programming. However, no two computer science or management information systems (MIS) programs offer the same complement of courses. The fundamental difference is that computer science (or computing science) is concerned with applications-independent (generalized) software, and MIS (or computer information systems, data processing) is concerned with specific applications. Computer science programs tend to concentrate on the hardware/software entity where MIS programs encourage a technical/business mix. For example, the computer science graduate might design and develop the software for a relational data base management system. An MIS graduate would use this software to design a corporate data base to support a variety of applications.

You should be aware that MIS and computer science are only two of a variety of possible computer-related disciplines. Others include computer engineering, software engineering, computer-aided manufacturing (CAM), and computer-aided design (CAD). Several of these have not matured to a full-fledged four-year curriculum.

The job prospects for each of these disciplines are excellent and will remain so for at least another decade. Ironically, the majority of those graduating in computer science are pursuing careers more closely allied with MIS (applications programmers and systems analysts versus systems programmers).

Even with the demand for applications-oriented programmers and analysts the way it is, there is a paucity of MIS programs. The problem is founded in a lack of understanding on the part of college and university administrators.

Sadly, most do not know the difference between a computer and a disk pack, much less be able to distinguish the subtle differences between the various computer-related disciplines.

Some computer science programs have tried to integrate MIS-type courses into the curriculum. Since most computer science professors have only a lukewarm interest in teaching COBOL or the fundamentals of structured system development methodologies, this format is seldom successful.

Another reason for the existence, or should I say nonexistence, of MIS programs can be attributed to the "chicken and egg syndrome." There are relatively few four-year MIS programs and even fewer at the graduate level. Consequently, only a few people are graduated with the "ticket" (a terminal degree). Those that obtain a doctorate are lured to industry by salaries that are almost double a professor's salary. If there are no professors, there will be no MIS programs, and consequently no graduates. I am certainly not advocating that industry lower their salary offers, but industry must recognize that the shortage of MIS specialists will persist until positive action is initiated by the industrial community.

Industry must reinvest in MIS education or risk losing their primary source of talent. In all fairness, industry has been generous in gifts of money and equipment, but the real shortage is people. An immediate solution to the university manpower shortage could be resolved through a "faculty loan" program. In such a program a company would "loan" a qualified employee to a college or university for a semester or up to two years. This is a small price to pay for the benefits that could be derived, both from education and industry.

Author's note: The next Q&A discusses MIS versus systems analysis and design curricula.

4.1.2.   Q. I just read your response to a question about MIS versus computer science college curricula (previous Q&A). Why is it there are so few colleges that offer degrees in business systems analysis and design?

A. Business systems analysis and design is a subset of MIS or information systems curricula. At the undergraduate level, the student would normally take two or three courses in systems analysis and design.

A few colleges still offer degrees entitled systems analysis and design, but I would expect them to be changed to MIS or information systems in the near future to reflect the breadth of the career field.

4.1.3.   Q. I was recently appointed to a committee to evaluate computer-related curricula at our medium-sized university. Even though there are more computing science than mathematics majors, computing science is within the Department of Mathematics. A few voices have proposed a separate Department of Computing Science, but the administration points to other computing science programs that have thrived in similar circumstances. Are we following the appropriate model for computing science education?

A. Even though computer/computing science is relatively new, it is already a well-established and rapidly-expanding discipline. Once a program has the faculty necessary to support a degree program, computing science should be afforded department status.

Computing science curricula evolved not only in mathematics departments, but in physics, electrical engineering, and other departments. In each case, there comes a time when ties with the parent department should be dissolved for the good of the university and the people it serves. Computing science should have the opportunity for independent growth.

4.1.4.   Q. After receiving my Ph.D. in economics, I took a faculty position in the school of business at a major university. I spent seven years in the economics department. Five years ago I took an interest in computers, transferred to the management department and began teaching courses in information systems.

We now have three professors with computer/information systems specialties and authorization to hire three more. We are having trouble attracting qualified people because the dean and the department chairs are reluctant to recognize information systems as other than a support function.

On numerous occasions we have approached the administration about consolidating information systems education into a separate department. They say that their primary concern is to strengthen the traditional areas. Do you have any wisdom that I can use to counter this position?

A. I question their wisdom. To maintain the attitude that information systems is a support function in a school of business is a step backwards. Smart business school administrators are paying a great deal of attention to the ordered growth of an information systems program. They recognize that a progressive information systems program is the best way to strengthen traditional curricula.

You may be aboard a sinking ship. If you do not detect a radical change in attitude by the end of the semester, I would suggest that you take a position elsewhere. There are plenty of openings.

4.1.5.   Q. I am one of two data processing instructors in the business school at a four-year college. At present, we only offer four support courses in DP. Recently we received funding for two more instructors and the dean has asked us to look into what it would take to offer a degree program.

We are considering adoption of the DPMA Model Curriculum for Computer Information Systems. How widespread is its acceptance? Do you feel that the curriculum provides an integrated and complete coverage of DP-related topics? If not, how would you recommend it be changed?

A. More people are seeking information systems degrees than ever before, but there is little or no uniformity between curricula. Traditionally, information systems courses have evolved because of the availability and content of a particular book or a professor's special interest. Few, if any, are based on a coordinated plan for information systems education.

The DPMA Model Curriculum is one alternative. The ACM curriculum is another. Currently, over 150 colleges and universities in the U.S. and Canada have adopted all or part of the DPMA Model Curriculum.

The DPMA curriculum is designed to prepare students for employment as business applications programmer/analysts. Its developers make a distinction between programs in business data processing, management information systems, and computer information systems. I submit that the distinction is a question of semantic interpretation.

The DPMA curriculum provides a good starting point, but I would not recommend its adoption as is. It is replete with redundancies, inconsistencies, and ambiguities. I would recommend that you address these shortcomings and add courses to the existing required list that will provide the student with a functional knowledge of data communications, database management systems, office automation, systems software, and state-of-the-art hardware.

I want to encourage the DPMA Education Foundation to make this curriculum an ongoing effort and to continue to provide colleges and universities with a leg up on curriculum development. The DPMA Model Curriculum would best serve the academic community if the course structure and the selected references were updated annually during these formative years.

Anyone interested in further details can contact the Data Processing Management Association Education Foundation, 505 Busse Highway, Park Ridge, IL 60068.

4.1.6.   Q. I work in the personnel department and specialize in recruiting and hiring people for our 600-person information resources department. Most are hired directly out of college and attend our training program.

Internally, the talk is of fourth-generation languages and the promise of enormous increases in productivity. However, the students that I interview usually have no more than an intermediate knowledge of languages like RPG, COBOL, and BASIC. Less than one in ten has any knowledge of fourth-generation languages. Why are our colleges not offering courses in fourth-generation languages?

A. I occasionally ask the same question of professors and they cite one or all of the following reasons.

1. It is not easy to make a major change to a curriculum that is already packed.
2. They cannot determine which of the many fourth-generation languages should be taught.
3. These languages are too costly for academic computer center budgets.

The first two objections can be overcome internally. The third is going to take cooperation from hardware and software vendors.

The trend in your organization and just about everywhere else is to use fourth-generation languages more extensively. College and university curricula that do not offer instruction in fourth-generation languages are falling behind.

4.2 COMPUTER LITERACY

4.2.1.   Q. I, along with 30 other middle managers, received a bluntly worded memo from the president of our company that encouraged us to become computer literate as soon as possible. Details were omitted.

Since I am the only middle manager with any semblance of computer knowledge, at least ten others have asked me for guidance. I consider myself to be computer literate, but the president's memo did not define it, so I am not sure.

At what level of knowledge does one become computer literate?

A. Companies promote it for their employees. Parents demand it for their children. Those who have it believe they have a competitive edge. Those who do not have it seek it out. "It" is computer literacy. Interestingly, in both business and academe, a fundamental question is often left unanswered: "What *is* computer literacy?"

Is it social issues, technical concepts, programming, application skills, and/or hands-on exposure to computers? If so, what is the proper mix?

I define computer literacy in terms of what an individual will have achieved upon attaining computer literacy versus identifying topics of study. You, as a computer literate person will:

1. Feel comfortable in the use and operation of a computer system.
2. Be able to make the computer work for you through judicious development or use of software.
3. Be able to interact with the computer—that is, generate input to the computer and interpret output from the computer.
4. Understand how computers are impacting society, now and in the future.
5. Be an intelligent consumer of computer-related products and services.

Author's note: My definition of computer literacy prompted a number of followup Q&As. Some of these follow.

4.2.2. Q. My boss handed me your definition of computer literacy (previous Q&A) and asked me to put together a program that would result in our middle and upper division management people becoming computer literate. I run an information center with a staff of three. About half of our intended audience have used our facilities at one time or another. However, I doubt if more than a couple would consider themselves to be computer literate.

I am concerned about our managers' willingness to devote time to attaining computer literacy. Before we get the program off the ground, we need to request a certain amount of time from our managers.

Could you give us some guidelines as to how much time will be needed?

A. A willing manager starting from scratch can expect to achieve computer literacy after about 120 hours of study and practice.

I would suggest that approximately 40 hours of that time be devoted to reading and study, interaction with pedagogical software, and some classroom or small group instruction. Another 40 hours could be devoted to developing skills in specific software, such as financial planning or electronic spreadsheet, that is specific to your organization and/or to their job function. The remaining 40 hours could be devoted to drill and practice in the use of available hardware and software.

I want to emphasize the importance of the last 40-hour segment. Any training on concepts and software that is not put to use is soon forgotten and never really appreciated.

Relatively few managers are willing to pull themselves away from their routine activities for 120 hours. As a compromise, propose that a 40-hour program be conducted during work hours over a two-week period. Then make computing resources and expert assistance available to them during both work and after-work hours so that they can complete the program. You will need to structure the latter two segments of the program with specific work challenges and deadlines, otherwise participation will die off quickly. The time spent on the self-paced portion of the program will, of course, vary considerably depending upon the managers' interest and willingness to learn.

4.2.3. Q. In a recent column (the first Q&A in this section), you defined computer literacy and raised a good point. Your definition was concise and usable as a beginning definition, but is computer literacy a fad or bandwagon upon which people hop without thinking?

The two most visible impacts upon society in this century have been the automobile and the computer. I have not, however, found any reference to an "auto literacy." I can make a few minor adjustments, such as pumping gas and changing tires, but when it really needs attention, I take it to an expert. I know a few buzz words, like "compression ratio," and I even have a vague idea of what they mean. This knowledge neither helps nor hinders me when I drive across town.

Computer literacy is relative. I am a data processing manager and could professionally stand to be more computer literate, but I know enough to be able to punch the keys on an automatic teller machine.

A. My definition of computer literacy must have struck a nerve in the computer community.

The analogy to auto literacy does not hold water. Those of us who drive automobiles take full advantage of their potential. When it is cold, we turn on the heater; at night, we turn on the lights; on the interstate, we drive the speed limit. A typical auto will have about 20 user-controlled options.

Computing hardware and associated concepts are much more sophisticated. A computer user may have thousands of control options. Computer literate people do not have to understand synchronous communications protocols, but they should have a basic understanding of the devices and appropriate associated concepts such as data management, systems versus applications software, and so on.

Perhaps the term computer literacy is a fad, but the concept is not. A person achieves computer literacy at a point in time. Part of becoming computer literate is learning that there is much more to learn. Unless a computer literate person retains some exposure to the dynamic field of computers, that knowledge is quickly lost or becomes obsolete.

Over 90 percent of the population between the ages of 21 and 65 are auto literate, but less than 5 percent of that same group can drive a computer.

4.2.4. Q. In your description of computer literacy (the first Q&A in this section), "Be an intelligent consumer of computer-related products and services" is the most important.

It is our responsibility in the computer industry to deemphasize computer literacy as a priority goal in our society. I would prefer that my son learn to think, feel, and understand than to find his precocity in the byways of the computer world. Likewise, I seek in a prospective employee one who can think analytically and creatively and can relate to other people in a sensitive manner.

The computer is a fine tool, but can't it be learned as needed to meet the tasks at hand?

A. You imply that computer literacy and learning to "think, feel, and understand" are mutually exclusive activities. Many agree with you. Although I agree that thinking, feeling, and understanding are worthy developmental goals, I contend that computer literacy can be a part of that development and perhaps even hasten progress toward other goals.

When you recommend that the computer be learned as needed, you are suggesting that we be reactive rather than proactive to a need for automation. I have always recommended that both computer professionals and users have a storehouse of knowledge that can be applied to a variety of situations.

4.2.5.   Q. Computer literacy happens to be one of my pet peeves, for exactly the reasons you cite (the first Q&A in this section): Nobody can define it but everybody is selling it. Your definition is as good as any I have seen, but it's nonoperational. Even after reading it, the computer illiterate still doesn't know how to go about becoming computer literate.

Computer literacy comes in different flavors. We computer professionals are computer literate, but this level of knowledge is not necessary for the ordinary computer user.

Then what are the necessary conditions for computer literacy? I believe that a necessary condition is an understanding of how a computer "thinks," with all it implies. In general, this means an understanding of the interconnection of hardware, the functions of the operating system, and the mechanics of software application.

In essence, what every computer illiterate needs is to attend a good seminar on "computer mentality." Do you agree?

A. Perhaps "computer mentality" may someday nudge out "computer literacy" as the term of choice, but both still address the issue of introductory computer education.

4.2.6.   Q. Is it just me, or is computerese having an increasingly greater influence on the way we communicate?

A. Yesterday, I **exited** the **port** at the **back end** of my **main** house and walked **through** the **gateway** to the **micro** shed **workstation** where I **retrieved** a few **productivity tools** for **maintenance.** My wife saw me **displayed** in the **window** and **transmitted** concern about the **density** of the grass.

I **interpreted** her **transmission** as a **command, booted** my **machine,** and **initialized** the **project** according to a **standardized methodology** that is based on a **top-down looping algorithm.** At **termination,** I **compiled** and **dumped** the grass on a **spreadsheet** at the **front end** of the **main** house. From there, a **common carrier uploads** the grass **overflow,** then **downloads** it to an **off-site location** for **permanent storage.**

Computerese may have impacted the communications systems of some people, but it is transparent to me and does not affect me a bit!

4.3 IN-HOUSE EDUCATION PROGRAMS FOR COMPUTER PROFESSIONALS

4.3.1. **Q.** For the last year and a half I have been assigned part time as a training coordinator. With almost no budget, there is little flexibility in what can be made available to our 65 professional people.

I was just appointed training coordinator full time and was asked to submit a plan for training and budget requirements. Which training methods have other companies found to be successful?

A. There is no one, two, or even three best approaches to information services education. The most effective education programs take advantage of all available sources of education.

It is your responsibility to recommend and direct personnel to the most cost effective alternative for each educational need. "Cost effective" does not translate to "cheapest." The following overview may help you to select an optimal mix of educational delivery systems.

- *OJT.* On-the-job training is a viable method of education if, and only if, there exists a well-documented set of learning objectives and a certain amount of time is set aside for the individual to pursue these objectives.
- *Independent study.* Provide the opportunity for independent study by maintaining an up-to-date library of books and periodicals. This is probably the most cost-effective approach for most circumstances.
- *Seminars.* If someone develops an expertise that you think could be of value to others, ask this person or persons to present an in-house seminar. A department your size should have

such a program every couple of months. Occasionally invite an outside specialist to lecture on a timely topic. There is an abundance of commercial seminars that are available in both public and in-house formats. Many of these are excellent. Since some are all marketing and no content, part of your job is to identify the good ones from the bad ones.

- *Video-based and computer-aided education.* The efficiency of the transfer of knowledge in self-paced education courses is a matter of debate. Even so, this relatively inexpensive approach to education should be part of your repertoire because of the range of topics that are made available.
- *University courses.* Seek out appropriate programs in neighboring colleges and encourage people to attend.
- *Conferences.* Every professional should attend at least one conference every year to 18 months.

4.3.2.   Q. My company has finally decided to make a commitment to education for MIS personnel. I have been asked to do some research and make recommendations for the training budget. The budget is to include a full-time MIS training director.

Are there any budget guidelines that others have followed in setting up an education program?

A. Because the scope of the training budget varies so much from organization to organization, I will speak in terms of education-weeks per year. Keep in mind that your choice of educational delivery systems has a major impact on a training budget. A week of self-paced video instruction is less costly than sending someone across the country to a seminar.

A surprising number—at least one third—of the MIS departments have no policy on education. In these cases, education is ad hoc, provided on an as-need, as-available basis. For those companies with an education policy, the average commitment is around two education-weeks per year per person. This figure is a bit misleading because many of these policies are not backed with implementation. I consider two weeks per year woefully inadequate, especially during a period in which we are experiencing such great growth in computer technology.

On the high end, it is not uncommon for some companies to fund eight to ten weeks of education for their technical people. Practically speaking, I don't see how any computer professional can hope to keep pace with the technology without devoting six to eight weeks a year to educational pursuits. I would recommend a policy that identifies a certain number of weeks, perhaps four, that would be dedicated to structured, interactive learning situations. This is to avoid the overused rationalization of on-the-job training. OJT is fine when properly administered and controlled, but most OJT is really OJW (on-the-job work).

Another couple of weeks should be set aside for individual learning that meets immediate needs for specialized expertise.

I recognize that many readers will pass this recommendation off as economically infeasible. But before you do, consider the potential for increased productivity (perhaps 100 percent or more) and the opportunities for a more effective use of the technology.

4.3.3.   Q. I have worked in technical systems for the past five years and have spent much of the past year learning about and installing local area networks. My boss has asked me to prepare and present a one-day in-house seminar on local nets.

My longest presentation to date is ten minutes and, frankly, I do not know where to start. Do you have any suggestion on effective presentation?

A. Let me highlight a few key considerations.

Prepare a detailed outline of the entire seminar for yourself, then condense it to a one- or two-page handout (idea processor software is an excellent tool for this type of activity). The act of preparing an outline causes you to crystallize your subject material into a logical sequence, and it gives the attendees a "road map" to follow.

Prepare examples that illustrate key points. You cannot have too many examples.

People not accustomed to speaking tend to underestimate the time required to present material. If you think that it will take 30 minutes, plan on an hour and you will be about right.

You will know local nets better than anyone attending, so exhibit confidence from the start. There is always at least one person that will attack at the first sign of instability. This person is more concerned about making you look bad than learning about local nets. Confidence is your best retort to this type of person.

Allow time for interaction, but never permit the discussion to drift away from the central focus of the seminar. As the seminar leader, you are responsible for directing the discussion. If you do not intervene, you may find the group talking about basketball rather than local nets.

Above all, have fun. If you appear to enjoy giving the presentation, then others will enjoy attending.

4.3.4.   Q. We have a very good training program for our programmers and analysts during the first ten months of employment. They are given formal instruction, video courses, and OJT. My concern is the OJT portion of the program.

The OJT guidelines do not permit us to use our trainees effectively. The guidelines distributed to me and other project leaders depict their role as primarily passive. In effect, they are to observe.

We hire good people and bore them to death for the first year and a half. I would like to get them involved in productive activities in the OJT portion of their program. What do you think?

A. I agree. As soon as they are educationally equipped to handle the task, make them a member of the pack. Throw them to the wolves.

4.3.5. Q. I manage a group of five overachievers. We have done our job so well that three of us are about to be transferred to less desirable positions. Our DP training center has been so responsive that our DP people and users are so well trained in the computer areas that they are requiring less ongoing training.

I would like to keep our training center at its present strength by selling our services to other companies. By doing this we would not be forced to dilute our ability to serve our own company. The vice-president of information services is not ecstatic about the idea, but he has asked for a proposal. Do you know of any other in-house training centers that have gone public?

A. I am aware of several in-house MIS education centers that service parent and sister corporations, but I am not aware of any that sell education on the open market. However, the idea is sound. Many companies would appreciate having the benefits of a full-service education center available to them while avoiding the headaches and the expenses associated with it.

4.4 IN-HOUSE EDUCATION PROGRAMS FOR USERS

4.4.1. Q. You once suggested that the key to having good interaction with users is having an ongoing DP education program for user management and analysts. As a training coordinator, I am responsible for all DP training. Presently, programs are geared to programmers, analysts, and DP management, but I would also like to implement a user program.

Could you be more specific about the scope and content of such a program?

A. The implementation of a user education program is the first step in creating an atmosphere of cooperation and understanding between DP and users. An ongoing program of in-house user seminars will help build lines of communication through a common understanding between DP and users, and between user departments. Not only is it necessary for users and DP to cooperate, but users must cooperate with each other.

A user seminar is much more than DP fundamentals. It also provides a forum for the resolution of problems and misunderstandings.

I have presented both public and in-house seminars for user personnel and, in my opinion, the in-house user seminar is the most beneficial approach to user education. This mode of presentation allows participants to interact with instructors and other users, all sharing the same environment and problems. A training coordinator, like yourself, DP managers, and other DP professionals can serve as instructors.

Depending on the company size, you might consider presenting seminars geared to the following levels: top management, middle management, operational management, user analyst, and clerical. Obviously, the content and approach to each of these seminars would vary.

Depending on the audience, the content might include MIS concepts, fundamentals of information processing, an overview of existing corporate application systems, corporate MIS policy and procedures, DP organization, user and DP roles and responsibilities, the DP plan for the future, the use of such software packages as word processing and spreadsheets, and other areas, depending on the type of organization.

I might add that very few programs exist, but as other data centers recognize the impact that having knowledgeable users has on improving user interaction, I would expect these seminars to be more popular than seminars on structured methods.

Author's note: In the next Q&A a reader with some experience in user education offers those considering such a program some solid advice.

4.4.2.   Q. For those readers who must provide user education, here are some ideas from which they might benefit. The going is still slow at times, but overall, our user education program is a success.

1. *Start small.* Don't overwhelm the participants with an all-day session.
2. *Demonstrate the benefit before teaching the technique.* Nothing interests people as much as showing them very quickly and dramatically how their work lives can be improved.
3. *Use a variety of teaching techniques.* Some people learn visually, others learn by hands-on experience. Provide several approaches.
4. *Don't make people feel foolish.* No one likes to appear inept, especially high-level managers. Use a nonthreatening teaching style. Give individ-

ual attention to those people whose skills are not up to the level of the rest of the group.

5. *Teach what they want to learn.* Interest is inspired best by responding directly to what your staff wants to accomplish.

6. *Offer an incentive for learning.* It would be wonderful to have top management say "Those who receive this training will get a raise," but this seldom happens. However, you might try scheduling your opening session as a luncheon.

A. You have made some good points; however, I am not in total agreement with the fifth point. In almost any user education program, there is a fundamental base of knowledge that users should have before they get "what they want to learn." The users do not always know what they want to learn. Another manager responding to this same issue wrote, "We don't start by teaching the users to program computers; we start with a computer awareness approach that familiarizes users with applications and resources of value to their professional involvement." I advocate this type of approach no matter what the learning objectives are for the user program.

4.4.3.   Q. My job is to provide user training for an on-line accounting system which has over 250 terminals at numerous sites throughout the plant. Most of the training sessions are composed primarily of clerical personnel with some training sessions including first-line management. I am constantly getting barraged with complaints about how the system "doesn't do this," it "shouldn't do that," or "here is a better way." People are really fed up and since I am available, they vent frustrations on me. Their complaints are not without merit—the system really does stink and there are no changes or enhancements planned for the foreseeable future. The fact remains I still have a job to do and cannot speak for 30 seconds without a hostile interruption. How would you handle the situation?

A. Contact your supervisor to determine if there exists a formal vehicle to document these complaints and ideas. In a company that size I'm sure such a procedure exists.

Don't step too far out of your job function, but no one would be harmed if you and your supervisor made an informal inquiry as to the last system evaluation. (My guess is it was the post-implementation evaluation, if any). If the system has been operational for more than one year without an evaluation, I would encourage the appropriate DP personnel to initiate such a review. Hopefully you will be able to tell your users of an upcoming system evaluation with the prospect of some positive enhancements based on their recommendations.

4.4.4.   Q. My staff and I give presentations almost daily to user groups, the systems advisory committee or management on topics ranging from technology updates to budget proposals. Most of the meetings are no longer than one and one-half hours. People have complained that we do not allow enough time for questions. How much time should be set aside for questions and answers?

A. The amount of time that you would allocate for interaction is directly proportional to the level of the audience. When making a presentation to top management, set aside about 60 percent of the planned time for direct interaction. Set aside 40 percent of the presentation time for interaction during mid-level management presentations, and 20 percent for presentations to operational-level personnel.

4.4.5.   Q. Five years ago, I purchased a personal computer for my home and quickly became interested in how I could apply it to my work. Seven years later I routinely use personal computers in my work as a product manager.

I am one of eight product managers in the marketing department, but I am the only one who actively uses computers. During the last few months, there has been a continuous parade of managers, including top management, stopping by to talk with me about how I am applying computer technology to my work.

On numerous occasions my manager has stated that he is proud of my work with computers and that he is very satisfied with my overall job performance. Ironically, he does not encourage the other marketing managers to use available personal computers as a tool in their work. I have never worked anywhere else, but it is hard for me to believe that our competition's managers would adopt such a laissez-faire attitude toward computers. Is this the case?

A. People say that this is the "computer revolution" and that we are entering the "age of information." This is true, but we are doing it more slowly than flashy television advertisements would have us believe.

Information resource management via computers is an attitude that must be nurtured—it doesn't just happen. It is hard to say whether your company is typical, but I would estimate that fewer than 15 percent of the companies in the United States have adopted the attitude that information is valuable and should be treated as a resource. In these companies, managers take every opportunity to encourage their subordinates to use the tools of automation.

4.4.6.   Q. In addition to my responsibilities as DP education coordinator, I have been assigned responsibility for end-user education.

My first attempt at end-user education was a failure. We announced and scheduled an eight-hour APL course to be presented on two consecutive mornings. There were nine confirmed reservations, and two showed up. Several called in and said they would try to make the second session.

I cancelled the course and have not rescheduled it or any other end-user program. Several users have asked me to try it again. Any advice on how to encourage end-user participation in these programs?

A. By cancelling the APL course, you made a tactical error. You turned away two people who had adjusted their schedules for an opportunity to learn APL. The best way to encourage future participation is to:

1. Do a good job in presenting the material.
2. Get some satisfied customers in the user community.

Complete the next course, even if only one person attends. Consider it an investment in user relations.

Before you decide on future end-user offerings, get them involved in the decision making. Invite their feedback on program alternatives. People are more willing to participate if they feel a part of the activity. Sometimes a carefully worded endorsement from a high-level executive is helpful.

4.4.7.   Q. What is the best way to teach integrated microcomputer software packages to users? We decided to standardize on a microcomputer and on an integrated software package. In support of our decision to standardize, we held three all-morning training sessions, each with about eight people (one to a micro). Using several predefined spreadsheet templates, we walked through two examples showing the major features of spreadsheet, word processing, data base, and graphics.

A month later, the micros we purchased for the various departments, as well as those that already existed, are basically unused. The managers are blaming us for their lack of use. They contend that the material was covered too fast and they forgot everything they learned. We had hoped that these sessions would give them a good start and that they would continue to learn through their own initiative. Apparently they made no further progress. Should we encourage them to learn on their own, or should we repeat the sessions?

A. Contrary to advertisements espousing the user friendliness of integrated microcomputer software, very few people, even computer specialists, can hope to gain much proficiency in a four-hour training session. Moreover, it is unlikely that they will retain much if what they learn is not applied shortly thereafter.

Plan to conduct another round of training sessions; however, this time allow more time. If your objective is to present these four software elements at a useful level of depth, plan on at least 16 hours equally divided between formal presentation and supervised practice.

As a follow-up, set up an information center so that advice and assistance are just a question away. As you know, if no help, or motivation, is available, all of the training will go for naught, and your new micros and software will continue to be unused.

4.4.8.   Q. I manage a small but apparently very popular information center. One of my duties is to present in-house seminars on word processing, spreadsheet, and data base packages. These seminars are typically scheduled on consecutive mornings and seldom last more than a total of eight hours.

Several managers have complained to me that the attendance of their people at these seminars places an unfair burden on the other people in the office. One manager has told his people that my seminars are off limits. Several managers have suggested that the seminars be scheduled during nonworking hours. Is it reasonable to expect clerical and professional staff to attend seminars before and after work?

A. Every organization should encourage and provide opportunities for professional development. Any white-collar worker who is not familiar with at least one of the three packages that you listed is not working efficiently. The seminars that you offer are solid investments in the company's future and I am surprised that management discourages participation.

Clerical personnel should be allowed to attend such seminars on company time. Off-hours seminars should be acceptable to progressive professionals.

part v

Career Planning and the Job Search

5.1 OPPORTUNITIES

Job Hopping and Job Stability

5.1.1. **Q.** I work in a staff capacity to the chief information officer of a Fortune 500 company. Both of us have strong personalities and irreconcilable differences. I have been successful with the company and hold a well-paying position but have no opportunities for advancement.

My boss would like to see me resign and for the last 18 months has done everything possible to make my life miserable. Will resigning affect my desirability as I search for a new position?

A. Conduct your search from a position of strength. Retain your position until you secure suitable employment elsewhere. You may be toiling under difficult circumstances, but you may be better off in the long run. It is much more difficult to obtain employment when you are "between jobs."

5.1.2. **Q.** There have been rumors for the past several years that my boss, the director of MIS, will be promoted to vice-president of MIS. It has not happened and I personally don't think it ever will.

Top management has openly voiced their displeasure with the performance of MIS. Their reluctance to promote the director indicates to me that they are not pleased with his performance either. It seems as though management has accepted MIS as a necessary evil with a mediocre manager. I see no changes on the horizon.

My concern is the careers of almost 50 people. Lack of technical progress and challenge has caused these careers to stagnate. Some of our best people have already left. Would you suggest I do the same or stay put and try to improve the situation here?

A. If it appears that a change of management and/or MIS emphasis will not be forthcoming within the next 18 months, then you should seek employment elsewhere. If there is a chance that you might get the job or the

149

director will be replaced with a capable person, then you might wish to stick it out so that you can take part in the turnaround.

It sounds as if top management and the director of MIS are taking a status-quo approach to the information revolution. Today's MIS directors cannot just sit back and take things as they come. Successful MIS directors keep top management continuously apprised of *all* alternatives, even those with political implications. Mediocre managers advocate middle-of-the-road positions.

The director of MIS is an agent of change, and, as such, should be willing to take a few risks. If the decision is made in the best interest of the company and someone in top management is politically offended, so be it. An MIS director needs to be aggressive, candid, and in constant interaction with top management. It is unlikely that your boss will suddenly acquire these qualities.

5.1.3.   Q. I hold a second-level DP management position in a Fortune 500 company. Marginal people in our department are being released, and the good people have already left or are looking for jobs. The company has not been profitable for several years and the outlook for the future is bleak.

My family is encouraging me to find another job. The headhunters tell me that they could place me in an equal or better position within three months. I would appreciate any insight you might have on my situation.

A. If others around you, especially top management, are trying to make a go of it, you might consider staying on. If your company emerges from the current difficulties as a leaner, stronger company and you are an active participant in the turnaround, then you may be rewarded with a quantum career leap.

On the other hand, if top management appears more concerned with their pension benefits than a turnaround, bail out.

5.1.4.   Q. Last January I resigned from a senior-level programming position of six years to make my fortune peddling computers. The job was definitely not for me and I left after two months. I would have left sooner but I could not find a position of commensurate pay. I was lucky. Three months ago I found an exciting, challenging, well-paying job.

A serious problem has arisen. A friend of mine has just offered me a job that sounds more exciting, more challenging, and offers a higher salary. I enjoy my present job and foresee a bright future with this company. On the other hand, I see the same opportunities in the other company. If I were to accept this job, would my work history record affect my future marketability?

A. Someone once told me that the grass is always greener on the other side of the hill, but I still don't believe it. Granted, the turnover in the computer business is very high, but four jobs in one year? This is inordinate and is bound to have a detrimental effect on your mobility should you decide to switch jobs again within the next three years.

At this critical stage in your career, a change in jobs is a calculated risk. If the next position falls short of your expectations and you begin to search for another position, a seller's market for everyone else could become a buyer's market for you.

Should you accept the position and remain with the company three or more years, you will have established some job permanence which would serve to negate the fact that you had held four jobs in one year.

Personally, I enjoy taking a calculated risk now and then, but it's not my decision.

5.1.5.   Q. Some years ago I made a mistake by leaving the data processing field to work in tool and die.

I have returned now and have worked in various DP shops, most of them less than state of the art. I have tried to improve myself by seeking an M.S. in computer science.

I have been unemployed for two months and am working with several EDP search firms and pursuing employment on my own. I lean in a technical direction. I know COBOL inside and out and am proficient in BAL. I also have tried to get into systems programming.

Unfortunately, I do not have extensive communications or data base experience, and the number of jobs I have held in the last few years has given me the appearance of being unstable. The only places willing to talk to me are all the same and I want to improve my situation.

I can't believe it! I'm always able to use my experience in helping junior programmers, but I can't seem to help myself. Am I already outmoded?

A. The grass is not always greener on the other side of the hill. There comes a time when you must establish yourself and prove to yourself and to your employer the potential of your contribution.

Contrary to popular belief, most computer centers are not state of the art. Base the selection of your next employer on whether you like the people and what you perceive to be the company's potential for growth in MIS. Be innovative and improve your skills by guiding your employer to new levels of sophistication.

After a reasonable period of time, you may wish to market your skills elsewhere, or you might enjoy the environment that you helped to build. After all, there is no law requiring MIS professionals to seek employment every 2.2 years.

5.1.6.   Q. As a data processing manager I do not believe that entry-level people are trained properly prior to employment. I also recognize that a high-potential entry-level programmer may be a cost-effective investment.

What is often overlooked is a new recruit's lack of appreciation for industry's expenditure of time, effort, and money on training. After obtaining training and experience, new employees sell themselves to another company. As a result, their benefactor is reluctant to invest in this effort again.

Management is hesitant to award substantial salary increases until the efforts of entry-level personnel bear fruit. But too often the patience and gratitude of the programmer are short lived.

Why should industry gamble with entry-level programmers when the odds of their rapid departure are so great?

A. A professional employee has an obligation to perform. An employer, and specifically management, has an obligation to challenge the employee and create opportunity. Those who leave within the first 1½ years do so, not for more money, but because they are not being challenged or do not see the opportunity for advancement.

If management neglects its obligation, then who can blame someone for seeking employment elsewhere? Management tends to view a trainee as nonproductive overhead for the first couple of years. The need for challenge and opportunity is no less acute during the training period than it is with experienced personnel. You can drastically change the odds of a rapid departure by confronting these high-priority personnel needs.

5.1.7.   Q. My husband and I work for the same company. He is in systems analysis and I am in accounting. A few days ago I was offered a position as an internal systems consultant. I was unaware that I was being considered for the position. With this job comes prestige and considerably more money, however, my husband was hoping to be promoted into the group in the near future.

The group's manager has assured me that if I accept the job my husband's chances of entering the group would not be affected. Their immediate need is for someone with an accounting background, so my husband was not considered for the current opening. My husband will support me on the promotion, but reluctantly. He feels that his chances would be diminished if I took the job.

I want to accept the job, but I won't if there is any chance that the move will adversely affect my husband's career. Do you have any insight into this dilemma?

A. Take the job. Opportunity doesn't always knock twice. Unique opportunities may come to your husband just as unexpectedly as they did to you.

5.1.8. Q. For the last eight years I have worked for a rapidly expanding regional computer services firm in the area of administration. To virtually everyone's surprise, especially mine, I was passed over for a promotion to vice president. My staff thought that I was the obvious choice, but a manager in software development was given the job. I am still convinced that I have a future with the company, but being passed over has delayed my career by at least two years. This position is my only opportunity for advancement in this company.

In the last few years the company's growth in personnel has surpassed our anticipated growth in business. To encourage a reduction in force, the company is offering a variable lump sum incentive to every management-level employee who resigns within the next three months. Mine would be almost $43,000.

I can get another job, but we would have to move to another city. What would your strategy be in this situation?

A. Since you were the "obvious" choice for promotion to vice-president, you can bet that your candidacy was discussed in copious detail. Apparently the powers that be have serious reservations about promoting you into the inner circle. Given the circumstances, I would encourage you to consider alternative employment.

5.1.9 Q. I am a senior programmer/analyst. I have worked for five different companies since graduating from college eight years ago. Each job offered a new opportunity and included a salary increase (in one instance, my employer went out of business). I have been with my current employer for about two years.

Another company has just offered me what appears to be a good opportunity with a substantial salary increase. Should I consider making another job change? Would another job change at this point in time damage my credibility in the long run?

A. As a rule of thumb, it is a year before a new programmer/analyst hire, even one with experience, begins to make a net positive contribution. Your current employment record has you leaving just after you start to have an impact on the bottom line. Because of this, your tenure with previous employers will overshadow your technical capabilities in future job searches.

If you take the new position, make certain that it is all that you anticipate. Plan on staying for at least three years so that you can reestablish your credibility as an employee. A prospective employer can only conclude from your current employment history that you may not be part of the head count in a couple of years.

Market Demand

5.1.10.   Q. The recent and enthusiastic interest in end-user computing, information centers, and user-friendly languages has made me a little concerned about my future, as well as that of thousands of other applications programmers.

If only half of the predictions come true, many of us will end the decade doing maintenance on batch applications that are too costly, complicated, or trivial to convert, or else we will be unemployed.

I'm not trying to start a campaign to abolish end-user computing, but can you suggest any areas of study or work that might help the applications programmers continue to be valuable to their employers? In other words, how do we keep our jobs?

A. Although it might compound your concern, I would be remiss not to remind you of the more universal applicability, availability, and acceptance of proprietary software packages.

Unless we as an industry reach a stalemate on imagination and innovation, applications programmers will be in considerable demand for some time to come. Look, however, for programmers and systems analysts to migrate to the functional areas as processing capability, data, and people are distributed throughout the organization.

5.1.11.   Q. My job title is Installations and Training Specialist. However, my job responsibilities are much more than that, and they include the following:

1. Design and implementation of user training programs.
2. User documentation of all systems.
3. Acting as liaison between the users and programmer/analysts.

With the diversified duties I perform, what would be the best job title to describe my function? Is this type of position in demand in the DP field?

If I want to stay involved in the user end of the DP field, should I be taking courses to learn programming?

A. You are currently the user education coordinator, user documentalist, and user liaison, and probably deserve a raise. The title most representative of the combined functions is the latter.

The user liaison function is critical to the success of any DP department. However, the scope of the function varies considerably from one company to the next. User liaison positions usually evolve internally. Companies seldom recruit externally to fill these slots.

I am a firm believer that a knowledge of programming is helpful, though not essential, in all DP-related positions.

5.1.12. Q. I am interested in pursuing an M.B.A. or Ph.D. in MIS. How is the job market for people with these degrees? Is the difference in salaries for Ph.D. and M.B.A. graduates significant for someone who has some MIS work experience?

A. The job opportunities for people with either of these degrees and MIS experience is excellent.

With regard to the M.B.A., your salary and success potential are very much dependent upon where you receive your M.B.A. An M.B.A. from one of the 50 top universities (several offer an emphasis in MIS) will give you some leverage during salary negotiations. With no experience and an M.B.A. from a prestigious university, expect to start in the low forties. Add the right combination of initiative, personality, and three or more years of MIS experience and you might start in the fifties.

Depending on your level of experience, a Ph.D. in MIS would put you in the $50,000 to $100,000 range in a corporate environment. Cut these amounts in half to determine the nine-month base salary range for an academic career; however, total compensation (consulting, royalties, seminars, etc.) for some professors surpasses that of their industrial counterparts.

5.1.13. Q. After a year's experience as a programmer, I am optimistic about my career, but will the demand for programmers and systems analysts continue over the next decade?

A. Look around you. How close is your company to implementing computer/MIS technology to its *full* potential? Even in the most sophisticated environments, we are only beginning. As I see it, the job functions may change with the technology, but the demand will be intact for at least 15 years and probably much longer. Any excess expertise will be quickly absorbed into the functional areas.

5.1.14.   Q. I returned to college to study programming and information services because of a recent career change. In a previous incarnation, I worked in sales and marketing. The reason I chose the computer field was the potential for jobs and career fulfillment.

At this point, neither seem attainable. I have availed myself to any type of computer-related position and have done everything possible to seek employment, from answering newspaper ads to sending out large mailings. And, always the same response: "Call us in two years."

Don't employers realize that they will soon run out of people with two or three years' experience? Has it ever occurred to these employers that recent college graduates could be an invaluable investment in their futures?

A. Recently I asked a roomful of MIS managers if they had openings for programmers or analysts. Then I asked them if they planned to fill these slots with experienced personnel or with recent graduates. All but one responded that they had openings, and all indicated that they were seeking only experienced personnel.

The problem persists, but hopefully not for long. Most said that they were having considerable difficulty recruiting qualified people.

The conversation that ensued painted a grim picture for those seeking experienced personnel. As we talked on, I and others touted the value of recent grads, and several vowed to return to the college market. I hope this starts a trend.

5.1.15.   Q. I have conducted several in-house training sessions over the last three years on database management systems and structured design. I enjoy teaching and would like to know what the career opportunities are in colleges and universities. Are there opportunities for part-time instructors?

A. Academe is experiencing a desperate shortage of data processing and computer science instructors. In all likelihood, you need look no further than local institutions to find openings. Recruitment of both full-time and part-time faculty has become an ongoing task in most departments.

At face value, academic salaries are usually not competitive with those of industry. However, for the right people, the intangible benefits more than make up the difference in pay. To get a feel for the value of these intangible benefits, I would suggest that you teach part-time for one or two semesters before making this major career decision.

5.1.16. Q. Six months ago I became one of almost 100 programmers who are between 21 and 40 years old. My supervisor and most of the other team leaders are in their late twenties.

It seems that there are a great many people going into computer programming and that making computers a career is becoming increasingly difficult.

I am an aggressive career-minded person and hope to move up the ladder. However, I am concerned that people starting in the computer boom five to ten years before me will fill and hold the higher-level positions.

Will there be room at the top for people like myself who are just entering the computer field?

A. Most would agree that more people are entering the computer career fields, but the opportunities are expanding as well. You and other entry-level people must start at the bottom of the pyramid.

Sure, fewer people occupy each successive level in a pyramid, so what's new?

Keep in mind that computers and information services are not everyone's cup of tea. The attrition rate for those entering the computer field is high.

Even so, promotion to the next level on the pyramid is and will remain very competitive. A few are in the right place at the right time or have an ''in'' with management, but generally speaking, promotions in the computer fields are more a result of dedication and hard work than tenure.

I am confident that the ever-expanding opportunities for automation will continue to provide upward mobility for career-minded professionals.

Approaches to the Job Search

5.1.17. Q. A month ago I sent my resume to ten companies located primarily in the Midwest. I have not received one positive response; most companies have not responded at all. I recently acquired an M.S. in computer science and have three years' work experience. Are there any jobs out there? I am beginning to think there are not.

A. The economic situation has forced so many people to adopt the shotgun approach to job hunting that it has lost its effectiveness. The sheer volume of resumes, applications, and inquiries has caused personnel departments to handle correspondence more casually and in a less timely manner than they did a few years ago.

Lost in the shuffle are qualified applicants for real openings in MIS. I have directed people to companies that I know have MIS openings and they are told by the personnel department that the company is not hiring.

The personnel department must reflect the company line, which in many cases is a hiring freeze. When a partial hiring freeze is in effect, MIS openings are given low visibility, both internally and externally. Nevertheless, these openings do exist. You just have to get your resume to the right person, who is usually in MIS and is often delighted to learn of your interest.

I am already anticipating repercussions from what I am about to say, but if I were in your shoes, I would be more direct and call the MIS department to make sure that your resume is properly reviewed. My rationale: The logjam in personnel departments is real and will persist for an indefinite period; there are jobs waiting to be filled; and there are people, like you, ready to fill them.

5.1.18.   Q. This year I will retire from the U.S. Air Force after 20 years active duty, the last nine of which have been spent in various aspects of the data processing business (programming, systems analysis, data base management, system management, etc.).

Between now and my retirement, I will be actively seeking full-time employment for a second career. I plan on using the services of job placement agencies. However, I also plan to send out resumes to individual companies.

I have been wondering if anyone publishes a directory or catalog of users of computer systems, and if so, how I might obtain one. A catalog such as this would be very beneficial in my quest for employment.

I would be particularly interested in a directory of computer users in the state of Texas, since that is where I would like to live and work.

A. Such lists and directories do exist but are most appropriate for vendors. These would be expensive and overwhelming for your purposes. I would recommend that you select a city or cities where you would like to live, then write the Chamber of Commerce and ask for an industrial directory, which includes company size, type, and contact person. Correspond directly with those companies that appear promising.

5.1.19.   Q. I am a systems programmer in the area of systems performance and tuning. I have decided that my talents could be better used elsewhere. Although this does not present a problem because I am as tired of this town as I am of my job, my problem is finding an organization that is looking for someone with my qualifications. I am receiving newspapers from cities I would like to live in, but it seems that large organizations looking for systems people do not place ads in the paper.

I have also tried finding a new opportunity through headhunters. It has been my experience that these people:

1. Always call at the wrong time and never when they promise to.
2. Talk your ear off for two hours and pretend to be interested in your personal life just to make conversation.
3. Ask silly questions like, "How many lines of code have you written in the last 14 months?"
4. Have little, if any, knowledge of what a systems programmer does.
5. Get their nose out of joint and say you are an underachiever when you say that you do not want to live in East Awfulgosh.

Is there any way for people who don't write COBOL or BASIC for a living to further their careers? I am on my fifth headhunter now. Should I try others until I find one that can fill my needs?

A. Placement agencies provide a valuable service, but they are certainly not the only solution. If your systems programming experience is with state-of-the-art hardware and software, you should be able to work anywhere you want. Companies everywhere, especially large companies, are forever looking for qualified systems programmers. Select the area or areas of the country in which you wish to live, then select particular cities. Write the Chamber of Commerce of these cities and request a membership list. There is usually a nominal charge for this list, but it contains exactly the information you need to identify potential employers.

If you are adamant about limiting your search to "large" companies, pick only those companies with 700 or more employees. Be advised, though, that smaller companies need good systems programmers also. Certain small organizations are far more sophisticated in their application of computer technology than some Fortune 500 companies.

Call the personnel departments of those companies that interest you and ask to speak with someone who deals specifically with employment in the computer-related areas. Request the appropriate paper work and correspond directly with this individual. "Dear Sir" letters get considerably less attention than those addressed to a particular individual.

Another way to get attention is to place a notice in the "Position Wanted" section of the classified ads. The "desperate" stigma long associated with this section no longer applies. Many career-oriented people in the computer fields find the "Position Wanted" section a convenient and anonymous way to advertise their desire for alternative employment.

Contract Programming

5.1.20.   Q. Several of my programmer friends and I would like to strike out on our own and do contract work. We're all fairly aggressive. Do you think we can drum up business on our own or should we go with a contracting service?

A. If you have the interest, skill, and ability to market your services, why not give it a try? After a few months you will know if you like this aspect of contract programming and if you are good at it. If you spend all of your time in nonbillable marketing activities, then perhaps you should exchange a percentage of your fees for contract leads and sign an agreement with a contracting service.

5.1.21.   Q. I am taking a special early retirement as a COBOL and PL/1 programmer. I would like to take occasional jobs on a contract basis after my retirement. How would I go about making such contacts?

A. First, you need to identify the potential market. Small companies often contract with individuals for both software development and implementation of packaged software. Medium and large companies contract for part-time or temporary help for augmentation and workload leveling.

Prepare a resume that emphasizes your most salable assets—availability, experience, desire for temporary work only, and so on. Send exploratory letters with a brief background description to data processing managers of a few local corporations, both large and small. Indicate that a resume is available upon request. Join and attend meetings of local DP professional associations. I have seen handshakes on several short-term, one-person contracts before dessert was served.

I have a warning and a recommendation. You should be aware that your services will be needed because a company is in a bind. More than likely, the work will be intense over a short period of time (every working day) versus being spread out over a longer period of time with part-time work.

5.1.22.   Q. My husband is a professor and teaches COBOL programming. I am also a COBOL programmer. We would like to try contract programming, on a limited basis to start. We would appreciate your advice on what kind of companies to approach and how.

A. To get started you will have to step out of the mold of a COBOL programmer. You have to make people aware of your skills and availability.

In part-time contract programming, *you* are the marketing rep and therefore, must sell yourself and your services to potential clients.

With a little persistence and a small investment, you can inform people of your availability via word-of-mouth, telephone, and personal letters. As to what kind of companies to approach, leave no stone unturned. Within the last two weeks the owner of a small appliance store and the director of a computer center with over a thousand people told me they were having a difficult time finding qualified contract programmers.

Placement Services Firms

5.1.23. **Q.** My problem is headhunters. They have done me more harm than good. Some headhunters send resumes to every company they can think of. When the company finds that it has resumes from more than one headhunter, it automatically rejects the candidate to avoid headhunter disputes.

I had asked the two headhunters with whom I had been working not to send a resume to a certain company because I had approached that company myself. Both headhunters sent resumes to that company and the company told me to reapply after a year.

Eventually I had to postpone my job search for a year. I did not use a headhunter when I resumed my search.

Is it reasonable to insist that a headhunter supply a list of companies contacted? I do not want one headhunter letter to nullify one sent by another.

A. What you can request is a function of your relationship with the search firm. That relationship is negotiable and it is up to you to lay out the ground rules during your initial conversation. If you cannot agree, look elsewhere for a search firm. If you give them carte blanche to distribute your resume as they see fit, you should request a list of companies to which your resume has been sent. Certainly, if there are companies that you wish to be off limits, supply the search firm with the list and update it as needed.

Author's note: In the next Q&A a search firm executive offers definite ideas on how to proceed, given the circumstances mentioned in the previous item.

5.1.24. **Q.** I am responding to a letter in your "Turnaround Time" column (previous Q&A) in which a disgruntled person was complaining about the treatment he was receiving from a headhunter. The nature of the complaint arose out of the agent's lack of respect for the candidate's wish that the agent contact a certain firm.

It is unforgivable for any agent to disregard the wishes of the candidate he or she represents. A candidate should never work with an agent who will not respect a legitimate request. Tell the agents what you expect, and send them the demand in writing. If agents do not acquiesce to this demand, turn them in to the governing state agency.

In the many years we have been placing computer professionals, we have never sent a resume until we first get in touch with our candidate and have determined that we have a mutual agreement that the position is suitable. Technically, the resume belongs to the candidate, and we treat it as such.

Please inform your readers to demand that their agents inform them prior to sending resumes and that they work as a team. If agents will not agree to these terms, dump them. You do not have to get stuck with a headhunter who is out to make a placement at any cost. There are plenty of us who respect the people we represent.

A. It is unforgivable for many professionals—lawyers, computer specialists, and a host of others—to do what they do, but they do it anyway. They will continue to do it as long as we let them get away with it.

I invite any readers who feel that they have been treated in an unethical manner by a search firm to let it be known. Let's see what can be done to eradicate the unethical elements in this business.

5.1.25.   Q. I have worked with a commercial software company for almost ten years. Two years ago, I changed jobs from creating software to marketing it. Yesterday, I received my first call from a headhunter, presumably because one of my products has been very successful this year.

She told me that a well-known software company was seeking someone with marketing experience. She felt that with my track record I would probably get the job if I interviewed for it. The position pays 50 percent to 70 percent more than my current salary. Although I am happy here, my wife and I are very enthusiastic about the possibility of a large jump in income.

I have no experience in dealing with headhunters and do not wish to discuss this with my friends at work. Does a headhunter really know whether or not I will get the job? Is this position too good to be true?

A. Search firms present candidates for consideration. One method of finding candidates is the blind call. She does not even know whether you will be invited for an interview, much less get the job. I would guess that there really is an opening and that the salary range was portrayed accurately. For the more traditional technical positions, however, this is not always the case.

5.2 CAREER MOVES

To Programmer, System Analyst, and Other MIS Careers

5.2.1. Q. I graduated with a computer science degree six months ago and took a job as a programmer. I just received my first performance review; my supervisor told me that I was doing excellent work and learning fast.

While everything seems to be going well on the surface, I may spend several days in front of the tube without coming up for air. I feel isolated and would prefer to do work that involves more personal interaction. I would like to stay in a computer-related career field, but not in programming. Can you suggest other positions that would give me more opportunities to work with people?

A. Being a programmer does not necessarily imply the working life of a hermit. Quite the contrary—a programmer's isolation is more often than not self-imposed.

The most effective programmers have frequent interactions with members of their project or maintenance teams. Peer review and user input are integral to successful software development.

By not encouraging interaction with more senior programmers, it is apparent that your supervisor is not giving you proper direction. During the first year of employment, a programmer needs and deserves more guidance. Express your concerns to your supervisor.

Your decision to give up on programming is premature. Given the proper environment, programming offers opportunities for personal interaction and career challenge. I would recommend that you give yourself an opportunity to mature as a programmer (a minimum of two years). Then, armed with a valuable programming background, you can transition to systems analysis, data base administration or any of a half dozen other computer career fields.

5.2.2. Q. Can you give guidance on career plans for people employed as DP policies and procedures analysts? Some friends who are technical writers are working in these fields and would like to become more informed about their work potential.

A. The responsibilities of policies and procedures analysts range from technical writers who copy edit MIS manuals to persons who work directly with top management in establishing and documenting MIS policy. Persons holding positions with such titles are usually in transit to and/or from a more traditional MIS function.

Experience in the more traditional areas is paramount to being successful as a policies and procedures analyst. For this reason, I see the career path of successful policies and procedures analysts overlapping with these functions.

For example, a technical writer with no systems or analytical background has limited upward mobility. A career path wholly within the policies and procedures area may be five to eight years away.

In the search for increased productivity, thousands of MIS managers have simply overlooked the implementation of MIS policies and procedures as a strategy to increased productivity. I have seen multinational corporations with no written policies or procedures. Certainly the work potential for such analysts is there, but recognition of the need is not.

5.2.3.   Q. I am an EDP audit manager at a large diversified company. I have eight years in programming and operations and six years in EDP auditing. Although my salary has increased dramatically over the last six years, I am becoming increasingly disenchanted with EDP auditing as a profession.

I thought that EDP auditing would be the yellow brick road to an upper management position. I don't think so any more. DP professionals consider EDP auditors to be accountants, and financial/accounting people consider us DP professionals.

Some questions:

1. Do you consider EDP auditing a good career path?
2. How long should one stay in EDP auditing?
3. How difficult would it be for me to get back into DP?
4. Where do you think I should go from here?

   A. Some answers:

1. Yes.
2. Until it ceases to be economically and personally gratifying.
3. For you, easy. Try quality assurance, systems analysis, or management.
4. To another company that offers greater opportunity.

Information systems auditing is a relatively new discipline whose function is not well understood. This lack of understanding impedes lateral and, ultimately, upward mobility. As a manager, you should take it upon yourself to create an awareness of the information systems auditing function, then promote the positive aspects (and there are many) of greater internal mobility for yourself and your colleagues. Opportunity will follow.

5.2.4. **Q.** I am a field engineer; we market, install, and maintain software-based IBM compatible remote and local cluster controllers, terminals, and printers. In the course of travels, I am frequently in large computer sites and have become interested in telecommunication systems networking and design.

From the brief synopsis I have given you, would you please tell me:

1. What kind of background in hardware/software is required for entry to such a position?
2. What would be the most direct route to such experience (job hopping, OJT, outside formal study)?
3. Are the various professional seminars in networking worth exploring?
4. Can you recommend a course of study (degree related or otherwise)?

I realize that your column is primarily dedicated to programmer/analysts or other software-related management positions, but as a relative newcomer to the industry, my lack of experience has made even knowing which questions to ask (let alone getting answers) quite a task. Please try to steer me in the right direction, as I am currently considering an attractive offer and wish to know if the new position is a logical step.

A. In answer to your questions:

1. Thousands of degree-holding applicants with similar aspirations have made a bachelor's, and in some cases a master's degree, a prerequisite. Those without degrees and holding such positions have advanced through the ranks via OJT and supplementary professional training.
2. If you do not have a degree, perhaps the most direct route would be a small company needing your hardware experience and willing to provide growth opportunities for you in telecommunications. The other less direct route is, of course, formal study.
3. Attendance at networking seminars will always be a plus but should be supported by experience to be of any value in the job market.
4. The obvious recommendations are computer science or information systems; however, check the program very carefully to insure that telecommunications and networking are part of the course of study. Some programs neglect this area in favor of more esoteric areas.

5.2.5.   Q. I work in a typical DP shop as a programmer/analyst and have been exploring other employment opportunities. I've been offered a job as an analyst for a company that manufactures its own special-purpose computers. Not only is the hardware unique, but so is the high-level programming language used. The job offer is very attractive, but would I be locking myself into a specialized narrow field?

If this job doesn't work out, will I be able to get back into the mainstream of data processing?

A. Surely you should be able to determine whether or not you like the job within two years. If anything, I expect the demand for experienced programmer/analysts to be even greater in two years. After a few months of review, you should have no trouble transitioning back to data processing, if you so desire.

Approach your new position with vigor, not with the idea of eventually returning to DP. If it does not work out after a sincere effort, you know you have another option.

To Management Positions

5.2.6.   Q. During the last 25 years, I have advanced to a position of MIS responsibility with over 100 people under me. I enjoy my job and would like to continue to advance within the company. But, there is literally no room at the top.

Given this situation, I released my name to a search firm who immediately got me an interview and an outstanding job offer from another company.

Here is the problem. I could stay here and perhaps stagnate in my current position or, if I am promoted, I would most likely end up with about double the responsibility of my current job offer. If I took the job offered by the search firm I would be number one in MIS in a much smaller company. If I leave the company and if tradition prevails, I would have no opportunity to return to my present company. If I remain in my present position, I may have a one in four chance at the top slot, but not in the near future. Any insight would be appreciated.

A. I could never recommend that someone wait for career opportunities to happen. Fast burners create their own opportunities, then take advantage of them. You could spend the remainder of your career waiting. Do you want a new challenge or do you want to wait?

5.2.7.   Q. I am presently working as coordinator of change management for a centralized systems department of a large corporate health care facility. The department handles data processing for ten hospitals in four states. The department has grown in only four years from 25 employees to almost 100.

My background consists of maintenance and development COBOL programming. For the last year and a half, I have been working in the area of problem and change management.

Within that time I have helped to develop and implement problem and change management functions in our company. However, I realize this is only a small part of the systems management field. Because of this, I would like to know:

1. What future is there for someone working in this area (problem and change management) of systems management?
2. Should I concentrate on expanding my knowledge of the entire discipline of systems management?

In addition, I would like to know why there have been few, if any, position announcements for individuals working in systems management? Is the concept of systems management a recent development?

A. The term *systems management* evolved with the increasing complexity of systems after World War Two, but never really materialized as a separate career path. The principles of systems management should be part of any manager's arsenal of management tools.

You cannot disassociate problem and change management from the basic precepts of management, especially in the computer/information systems area where grandiose changes are commonplace and problems are part of the routine.

A knowledge of the considerations and approaches to systems management is valuable, but not to the detriment of other DP management skills. The vast majority of organizations are looking for managers with skills to cope with all facets of the DP environment, not just problems and change.

5.2.8.   Q. In five years with a Fortune 500 company, I have been promoted three times and am now a project leader. Of course, I am not privy to all information, but from what I have seen in the past year or so, promotions from project leader seem to be random.

How does a person in my position break out of the pack?

A. As I have noted before, hard work and a quality end product seldom go unnoticed. However, you should become keenly aware of the company's personnel performance criteria, evaluation methodology, and what is expected for promotion. Set objectives that, if accomplished, will meet these criteria. The realities of promotion dictate that you also be politically astute and avoid unnecessary confrontation.

Punch one more ticket than your colleagues (e.g., CDP, master's degree, speaker at a major conference). Maintain a state-of-the-art knowledge of computers and information systems by reading related journals, periodicals, and books. This knowledge and understanding will surface in meetings with your managers.

Perhaps the best way to be noticed is to be imaginative and innovative. In the process of accomplishing your job function, make note of any procedures, methods, systems, and so on, that could be improved. On your own time, identify the problem and develop a generalized solution. Present the idea to your immediate manager. If the idea is not accepted, drop it immediately and keep looking; if the idea is liked, offer assistance in expanding or implementing it. In either case, you win.

In any highly competitive situation, the promotions are afforded those who are not only good at what they do, but are willing to go beyond the call of duty.

5.2.9.   Q. For seven years I have been with a consulting firm where each promotion is an up-or-out decision. My last two promotions have been on time and my supervisors have indicated that I am doing what is necessary to eventually be considered for partnership.

A few recent events have caused me to rethink my career. Two very competent colleagues were denied partnership. This came as a surprise to everybody.

In addition, I have been offered an MIS management position with a client company that offers excellent advancement opportunities.

Given the inconsistency of evaluation criteria at my firm, would you suggest that I resign and take the position at the client company?

A. You are confronted with resolving the age-old question of risk versus security.

If you enjoy consulting and aspire to partnership, and you feel comfortable with your progress towards that goal, pursue it.

If you feel that ambiguous performance evaluation criteria preclude you from shaping your career destiny with good performance, perhaps you should leave the firm.

5.2.10.   Q. My husband is currently a systems manager at our company's headquarters office. I work as an administrative assistant in the personnel department. My husband was recently offered a promotion with a 50 percent increase in salary, but we would have to move to a regional office in the Midwest.

Under normal circumstances, the company would be willing to transfer me as well, but since my husband will be over all departments that would hire secretaries and administrative people, they said that I would not be able to transfer to that office.

My husband wants to go, but I have second thoughts. If they can transfer other husband-and-wife teams, why not us?

A. Most companies will not permit a situation where one spouse can in any way influence the performance evaluation of the other. It may be a while before opportunity knocks a second time for your husband. If he turns down this position because you will not be retained, company executives will consider his decision to be poor judgment and will be reluctant to offer such a promotion in the future.

5.2.11. **Q.** After 13 years of moving up through the ranks of several DP organizations, I feel that it is time to move into a No. 1 or No. 2 spot (director or assistant director of DP). How does one find such openings? Most of the ads are for the lower-level positions. Are there reputable placement agencies that specialize in these jobs? If so, how do I find out about them?

A. It stands to reason that the number of job opportunities for directors or assistant directors of DP would be somewhat less than the number for the lower-level positions, and so it is with the listings of professional placement agencies and the positions announcement section of *Computerworld*. Checking the *Computerworld* classified section for four consecutive weeks, I counted an average of ten DP director positions per issue. All DP placement agencies that I contacted assured me that they had listings for the top spots.

These positions are available, but my experience has shown that the vast majority of these positions are filled from within or via internally generated recommendations. In your case, I assume an internal promotion is unlikely, for whatever reason; therefore, I would suggest that you make yourself known through informal conversations at local professional society meetings, major regional and national conferences, professional seminars and perhaps by publishing articles in DP periodicals.

To my knowledge, no DP placement service specializes in listing positions for director or assistant director. You did not indicate your present position or size of your installation, but in order to broaden the scope of potential job opportunities, you might consider a move to a larger installation as director of programming and/or systems and use this position as a steppingstone.

Be advised that the scope of the job function of the assistant director varies considerably from one company to the next. The assistant's job function may vary from routine administrative tasks with no line authority to actually managing and controlling the DP department.

Author's note: The next Q&A is a follow-up to the preceding Q&A.

5.2.12.   Q. I just read your answer to the person who wanted a No. 1 or No. 2 position in a DP organization (previous Q&A). I, too, have over 14 years of DP experience, the last seven years as an operations supervisor. I am 33 years old and have many years of my career ahead of me. Your recommendation was to possibly use director of programming or systems as a steppingstone. Why is systems and programming always the key to DP directorship? I do systems work and have done extensive programming over my career. I even teach DP at the local community college. Are you suggesting that I cross over to systems and programming in order to reach my goal of DP director?

A. Systems and programming is not always the "key" to securing the No. 1 information services position. Operations managers have also had success in being promoted to the No. 1 slot. However, since systems and/or programming managers are exposed to more facets of DP and are closer to the needs of the organization, most internal promotions come from these positions. Hard realities dictate that an operations manager seeking a one-jump promotion to DP director may have to look outside of the company or, internally, in a smaller satellite facility.

5.2.13.   Q. I am a student majoring in business administration, specializing in business information systems. I am currently working in a small installation in the capacity of supervisor of computer operations. I need your help to establish a career path to follow. My career objective is to become a DP manager, but I have little experience in programming. Does one need to be knowledgeable about programming and/or data base design to become a DP manager?

A. A DP manager should be knowledgeable, but not necessarily experienced, in programming and data base design. The successful manager will also have a working knowledge of all major facets of information services, to include systems design, auditing, operations, project management, and a dozen other areas of equal importance.

Of the hundreds of MIS directors that I have met over the years, I can count on one hand those that have *not* had any programming experience.

To Consulting Careers

5.2.14.   Q. I recently received a bachelor's degree in management information systems and am currently working as a COBOL programmer. I enjoy working with computers but would prefer to work more with people.

I would like to work as a type of consultant. What experience and education do I need? I have been told that I would get better experience through sales than systems analysis.

A. A good consultant has a wide range of experience and exposure to a variety of situations. I can think of only one other position that would top a systems analyst for experience and exposure. That position is, of course, a consultant. However, very few consulting firms hire rookies. Get three or four years of experience and perhaps a master's degree, then seek a position as a consultant.

5.2.15.   Q. A friend and I are considering resigning our current positions with a large company and going into the consulting business. Between us, we have 25 years of business programming experience. Both of us have excelled in a variety of programming languages and feel that we are qualified to develop and program just about any kind of system.

We are new at this and would be interested in any ideas that you would have that would help us to get started. What should we charge as an hourly rate for programming?

A. I don't mean to dampen your enthusiasm, but you are going to have a lot of competition. The work is there, but don't expect a flood of clients the moment you open for business. Be prepared for some lean months during the first year.

Unless you are independently wealthy, try to secure reasonably steady work for the first five or six months prior to resigning. Use this work as leverage to get more work. You can test the water through casual conversations at professional society meetings and with close friends.

Don't blatantly hang out your shingle before notifying your employer of your resignation. It may backfire. You and anyone else in similar circumstances have an obligation to your employer. Make sure that your current projects are clean, well documented, and can be easily transferred to someone else for completion.

Once you establish your company, don't forget that one of your primary functions is marketing. No accounts, no work, no pay. Increase your visibility in your community and surrounding area. Don't miss an opportunity to inform potential clients of your availability.

The hourly rate for contract applications programming is a function of geography and the prestige of the company. Rates vary from $25 to $70 per hour. Ironically, the correlation between program quality and the level of the fee is a matter of debate. Some large prestigious companies charge out rookies at the high end and some small companies offer experienced personnel at the low end. Geography notwithstanding, I would consider $25 per hour an absolute minimum.

5.2.16.   Q. I would like to plan for a career as a DP consultant specializing in office automation. I have four years experience in planning and am currently involved with minis and micros in office automation. What are the rewards and pitfalls for consultants in office automation?

A. The demand for good office automation consultants is and will remain high. The problem is that anyone who has sold, used or seen a Displaywriter has become a consultant and proclaimed himself or herself an expert in office automation. As a result, the good consultants have a tough time convincing confused buyers of their worth.

An office automation consultant should have a specialized expertise to market. The good ones will have an in-depth knowledge of how to integrate existing computer-based systems with the various facets of office automation.

The most difficult problems faced by office automation consultants are not technological. They are computerphobia, the reluctance of secretaries to part with their typewriters, management's resistance to learning keyboarding skills, and convincing top management that office automation deserves a higher priority. If you have the technological skills, the ability to integrate, and can successfully cope with these attitudes, the rewards are high.

With so many "experts," the most common pitfall is to sell expertise that you don't have. Sooner or later you have to produce.

5.2.17.   Q. I am considering a career move from the government sector to industry or consulting. My academic background is strong and includes a B.S. (and almost an M.S.) in computer science. Following my undergraduate education were six years of DP experience split evenly between solid programming experience and teaching experience in everything from COBOL to software methodologies.

Three years ago I moved into non-DP administration and decided to keep my hand in DP by pursuing a master's degree. I lack COBOL or financial systems experience, but am very interested in the area of information management. My forte is dealing with non-DPers. I enjoy the small projects that offer variety.

I will climb down from my lofty federal salary, if necessary, if I could find a 30-hour per week or part-time opportunity that would enable me to have more time with my family. Where should I begin and what should I expect to find?

A. I can sympathize and identify with your desire for a shorter work week. Unfortunately, my creditors see things differently.

Your credentials are reasonably impressive. How about starting your own company? You could go it alone or join forces with one or two other people. Many small companies are seeking the kind of advice and assistance that you can offer. If you are persistent, you may reach a point at which you can trade billable time for family time.

Most of the part-time opportunities are for work-force augmentation and involve programming. Since this does not parallel your interests, starting your own company may be your best hope for a 30-hour work week. Be prepared, however, for an intense effort on the front end.

To User Areas

5.2.18.   Q. My marketing group, which consists of five product managers, myself, and three administrative assistants, bought a micro about two years ago. It sat idle for more than six months and, finally, my manager asked me to learn how to use it.

I attended a two-day spreadsheet seminar and returned more confused than informed, but during the next month, I spent just about every waking hour in front of the computer or with a manual. A year and a half later I am the company's micro "expert." The people in MIS refer all micro questions to me.

I am still a product manager, but effective use of the computer has cut the time I used to spend on the job in half. Most of my time at work is devoted to assisting people in my group and in other groups with their particular micro needs or problems. I do nearly everything from education to setting up templates, but I do not enter someone else's data.

My unofficial microcomputer activities are actually encouraged by management, but I am evaluated strictly on my performance as a product manager. I find myself enjoying my work with computers much more than my job as a product manager. My current project involves networking the micros in my group.

I'm considering a career change to the computer field, but I don't know where to start. My present employer has been good to me, but I don't think I would enjoy working in our MIS department. My degrees are in business; do I need a computer-related degree? Is there a demand for someone like myself?

A. There is a tremendous demand for people with functional-area expertise and home-grown computer talents. In not too many years, the majority of computer professionals will be organizationally attached to user groups, not a central MIS department. To be sure, there will be centralized control, but just about everything else will be distributed to the user areas, including people. The point is, you do not have to be affiliated with an MIS department to be a computer specialist.

Express your desire to pursue a more computer-oriented career to your manager. I would be surprised if your manager, or perhaps someone higher up, doesn't jump at such an opportunity. If they don't, there are a thousand marketing managers who will. The typical product manager in marketing still spends at least four hours every day laboriously seeking information that, with a little forethought and a micro, could be obtained in an hour.

If you wish to continue full-time work with micros in a user area, an occasional continuing education course and plenty of reading will suffice. A degree in computer science will be of marginal value.

5.2.19. Q. Three years ago my boss bought a microcomputer and it sat idle for six months. I was, and continue to be, the only one interested in using it. During the past two and a half years, I have taken at least one computer science course per semester and have installed several small applications on the micro at work.

In my current position, I spend no more than one day a week with the micro. Another user department and our DP department have both offered me positions that would allow me to work full time on computer-based projects.

The opening in the user department does not involve any development work, since all of their applications are supported by DP. They would like someone to do all of their spreadsheet work and generate one-time reports on their microcomputers. Requests involving mainframe systems would continue to be sent to DP. The opening in DP is a COBOL programming position.

I would feel more comfortable in the user department but would prefer the job in DP. Which do you think offers greater opportunities?

A. Many user-based positions offer technical challenge and career opportunity. The one you described does not. It sounds to me like they want a gopher. Micro applications, especially the interactive spreadsheet packages, are user friendly and designed for use by the decision maker. Asking an intermediary, like yourself, to obtain information from a spreadsheet is like asking someone to go to lunch for you. It just doesn't make sense.

If the user position does not offer opportunities to work with DP development and maintenance personnel, take the DP job.

5.2.20.   Q. Three months ago, I was a victim in a company-wide cutback. Although it is little comfort to me, data processing was not hit as hard as other departments.

I am attempting to find a DP position (any position) in the local area. My 22 years of DP experience have gotten me some interviews, but I feel my age (47) has ultimately been the determining factor.

Could you suggest a search strategy for someone in my position?

A. Even though you may be willing to take a job at the salary of an entry-level programmer, potential employers feel that, over the long run, this is not a workable situation. Put your maturity to work for you. Look outside of the MIS function to the user departments. Most user departments would prefer to hire someone like you in a user liaison capacity than some young "techie."

The year 1985 may well be the year of the user liaison (or business analyst or account executive). Although these types of positions have been around for some time, for the first time, user departments are recruiting such people in large numbers.

Check out opportunities in the user areas as well as MIS. And don't forget your old company; substantial company-wide cutbacks are often followed by the voluntary departure of many good people. I would expect that some of these openings will be filled with user liaisons.

5.2.21.   Q. Currently three marketing/advertising professionals and two secretaries report to me and I have authorization to fill an empty position with another professional. The job description calls for someone with experience or a degree in marketing, but what I need is someone with a solid computer background and an interest in marketing. The Personnel Department refuses to change the job description because they want to retain the same complement of personnel for all product marketing managers.

My group is paving the road for other product groups in the area of microcomputer applications. However, we are beginning to get in over our heads and need help to progress any further. A couple of DP programmers have been helpful, but the time they can devote to our microcomputer needs is very limited.

Everyone in marketing, including my boss, is very impressed with what we have done, but they do not know enough about computers to understand that we are on the verge of making some serious productivity gains. How do I convince my boss and the people in personnel that we need a micro specialist?

A. Tell your boss that within five years, more computer specialists will work in the user areas than in centralized MIS departments. Then ask your boss if your company can afford the luxury of bucking this trend, considering that the company will miss out on opportunities for productivity gains and, possibly, opportunities to gain a competitive advantage.

Those companies that refuse to change policy or revise the organizational structure to accommodate the trend of moving technical expertise closer to the user should be preparing to "play catch up" during the next few years.

5.3 CAREER DEVELOPMENT

5.3.1.   Q. I am a programmer in a large installation. This is my only job since getting my B.S. two years ago. Several of my peers are "pecking away" at getting a master's degree part time. Now I am beginning to think about it also. The company will pay tuition and give time off, but I am thinking more of my investment of time and energy.

Is a graduate degree of any value? Which degree is best?

A. A master's degree will, in the long run, prove to be an asset. However, the short-term worth of a master's degree is often dependent on management's views of how the degree program affects your job performance. For whatever reason, some managers believe your efforts should be concentrated solely on the job and not shared with a degree program. If your management thinks this way, a master's degree may actually work against you.

Not long ago the high school diploma was the norm. Now the bachelor's degree has become the standard entry-level prerequisite for many companies. The writing is on the wall. Companies are encouraging advanced degrees through tuition refund programs and more people are pursuing the master's degree immediately after graduation. Some day soon, expect the master's to be the norm.

As thousands of those with master's degrees will attest, one does not obtain a master's degree part time without sacrifice. Reports, projects, examinations, and attending class may take as many as five nights a week.

For you, now is probably a good time to return for your master's. You have two years of experience that you can relate to your classwork and you are not too far out of the regimen of academe.

No one degree is best for programmers in general. A master's degree program should be selected based on your background and future aspirations.

A systems and possibly an applications programmer might benefit from a degree in computer science; however, applications programmers might find some computer science programs too theoretical and of marginal value for application to their environment. If you wish to work in application systems analysis and design, a program in information systems would be helpful. Unfortunately, these programs are rare. If you ultimately want to go into MIS management, an information systems or M.B.A. degree would be best. Availability, however, is often the determining factor.

Author's note: In the next Q&A a reader offers some food for thought with respect to the preceding Q&A.

5.3.2. **Q.** In your reply to the question of graduate degrees (previous Q&A), you state that "no one degree is best for programming." Then you devote most of the rest of the reply to computer science and information systems degrees.

One of the biggest problems we face is communicating with our users who do not talk in bits, bytes, nanoseconds, and so on, but rather who talk in terms of debits, credits, inventory turns, expense analysis, budget variance and the like. Let's face it, a company can only stay in business if it makes money. Therefore, financial control is very important. I am not slighting the other areas of order processing, inventory control, engineering, distribution, and service. The point is that the degree should be in business because it gives a good introduction to the broad scope of business management and is particularly useful to the person who has a nonbusiness undergraduate degree. It introduces business terminology and concepts that are invaluable in dealing with a variety of users. The specific detail needed for solving a problem will be supplied by the user.

I recall a situation where a programmer analyst who knew very little about accounting attempted to solve a problem in the area of general ledger. The accountants knew what they wanted but their proposed solution was a disaster from a data processing viewpoint. When the situation was reviewed at the request of the programmer analyst, we worked out a different approach that gave the accountants what they needed, but at the same time reduced the programming effort required by eight weeks. Just knowing the accounting concepts helped a great deal in this case.

As for the reader's comment that his peers are "pecking away" at getting their master's degrees, Confucius said it best: "Even a journey of 1,000 miles starts with the first step." Get going, friend. I speak from experience, having received both my bachelor's and master's degrees at night.

A. Thank you for this opportunity to set the record straight. I am a strong advocate of DPers understanding not only the basics but also the intricacies of the functional areas in which they work.

Whether programmers seek advanced degrees in computer science, information systems or business is dependent on their background. Programmers should strive to obtain knowledge (or a degree) that provides the mix necessary to enable them to effectively communicate with users and to accomplish their job function.

Author's note: In the following Q&A another reader puts in his "two cents" on this topic.

5.3.3.   Q. After reading your reply to the question "Is a graduate degree of any value? Which degree is best?" (the first Q&A in this section), I cannot help but put my two cents in. The answer is definitely a Master's of Business Administration (M.B.A.).

In my capacity as a counselor and advisor to young people who work for me, my advice is to get an M.B.A., unless you are going to be a hardware or software specialist. The M.B.A. provides the education needed when you advance to management and must bridge the gap between DP and business.

A. As I have stated in previous responses, the graduate degree that one should seek depends on the individual's background, maturity, circumstances, career aspirations, and, of course, availability of degree programs. Although the M.B.A. is a viable option, it is not appropriate for all management aspirants.

I must take exception to your statement regarding the education provided by an M.B.A. because such programs, like so many corporations, have been slow to recognize the importance of management of corporate information resources. The typical M.B.A. program offers an introduction to programming and business systems. These subject areas should be handled like introductory accounting and made prerequisites for admittance, not part of the curriculum. The M.B.A. student should be exposed to strategic planning for information services, not FORTRAN.

M.B.A. programs have been derelict in course offerings in the area of information resource management. Awarding M.B.A.s without higher-level study in this area is akin to selling automobiles without steering wheels.

In all fairness, a handful of M.B.A. programs have sophisticated offerings in this area. To no one's surprise, they are the so-called "good" M.B.A. programs.

5.3.4.   Q. I would like to pursue an M.B.A. with an emphasis in MIS. Is there a list of universities that offer such degrees?

A. *The Official Guide to M.B.A.* (Education Testing Service, Princeton, NJ) contains a list of all the M.B.A. programs. In the guide, each program is cross-referenced to any of 15 areas of concentration, one of which is MIS. The guide is often available in college bookstores.

The criteria of what constitutes an emphasis or concentration in MIS is not clear. I am familiar with several of the M.B.A. programs that claim MIS concentration, and entry-level COBOL is their most sophisticated course. However, the guide gives you a place to start.

Have you considered pursuing an M.S. in MIS? Some MIS-oriented M.B.A. aspirants overlook this educational option.

5.3.5.   Q. I will graduate in June and eventually hope to work in the DP field. I am considering graduate school, but my advisor suggested that I get a job and devote my energies to working for a couple of years, then return to graduate school full time. I would appreciate your input.

A. Students often ask me whether they should stay for a master's degree or go to work. My response differs from one person to the next based on the individual's level of maturity, continued enthusiasm for academic work, the institution they want to attend, and other factors. If your advisor knows you and your circumstances well, you have probably been given sound advice.

5.3.6.   Q. I recently retired from the military. In order to be prepared for this time, I earned two B.S. degrees in business and data processing, and an M.A. in management. I have accepted a systems analyst trainee position with a progressive oil company.

I want to continue my education. My first thought was a masters in computer science, but now I am not too sure. My personal preference is in the management field.

What type of schooling would you suggest?

A. You have two bachelor's and a master's. Another master's degree will be of marginal value. Your best bet is to pursue continuing education in specific job-related skills.

Ask your supervisor what skills will be required during the training period. Direct your educational efforts toward acquiring these skills. This will accelerate your experience and, therefore, your progress toward management.

5.3.7.   Q. For the past seven years I have been involved in all aspects of the printing business. My undergraduate degree was in the social sciences, so almost all my DP training has been on the job. For the past three years I have been a DP manager for a $20 million magazine printer, and I manage a staff of two.

In order to be more effective in my current job and to be more attractive to future employers, I feel that I need some formal training in all aspects of MIS management. How can I improve my knowledge to be effective in my current job and to increase my future marketability?

A. Most MIS degree programs, at both the undergraduate and graduate levels, focus attention primarily on the use of and application of hardware and software technology. Topics such as programming, DBMS, and system design tools lend themselves nicely to the classroom setting. But the principles of MIS management are difficult to teach and learn outside the context of a particular set of circumstances.

As a result, academic institutions sometimes slight such topics as planning, procedures, in-house education, personnel management, and the implementation of productivity measures.

Effective MIS managers are seldom products of formal education programs. Certainly MIS managers wishing to improve their ability to manage take advantage of available educational videos, seminars, books, and periodicals. These resources provide them with a foundation of understanding for specific facets of the MIS management function. The real learning comes when they attempt to apply this knowledge to their environment.

When confronted with a particular management problem—information systems planning—the really good managers tend to immerse themselves in all available information on the topic. Then they make a concerted effort to apply what they have learned. In short, the overwhelming majority of practicing MIS managers improve their skills through self-study and good old on-the-job training.

5.4 PRESENTING YOURSELF TO POTENTIAL EMPLOYERS

5.4.1. Q. I am a computer professional with 20 years of experience in both teaching and programming. I can program in eight languages. I have been responding to newspaper ads for programmers and teachers for over six months and, in most cases, have not even received an acknowledgment of my inquiry, much less an offer.

I do not respond to blind ads; I do not consider these either professional or legitimate. My resume is in the hands of several headhunters from whom I have heard absolutely nothing. Once, I even reformatted my resume so that ten years of experience (and hence age) disappeared—no response to that either.

What's going on here? Am I unmarketable? If so, why and what can I do about it? I do not insist on holding out for the salary my experience might demand. I do not apply for a job unless I think I can do the work and accept an offer.

A. Something is amiss. You might be missing an important ingredient; perhaps a degree, management experience, or state-of-the-art knowledge. Or there is something about your resume that is turning off potential employers. I routinely come across resumes that are at best arrogant and at worst downright irritating. The writers of these resumes must have felt that they were putting their best foot forward or they would not have distributed them.

The resume is often the key to the door and should be compiled with great care, with the intended reader in mind. Little things can result in your resume being placed in the circular file. Here are some examples: A 1973 college graduate included his college grade point average; a "supersalesman" writes three paragraphs on his first job and two sentences on his last job; a recent college graduate inserted the company's name in pencil on a preprinted letter of transmittal; a systems analyst underlines his IBM 360 BAL experience; and the list goes on.

If in fact it is your resume that is giving you problems, edit it and pass it on to four or five people who you know will be candid in their assessment. With competition for jobs the way it is, the letter of transmittal and resume must be flawless.

5.4.2. Q. I was not affected by a recent work-force reduction, but the writing is on the wall. I will surely be cut in the next one. In preparation for the inevitable, I have begun my search for another position. I have responded to all ads in the local newspapers and have sent my resume to virtually all reasonably-sized companies within commuting distance of my home.

To date, I have not received one invitation for an interview. My resume is enclosed. I would appreciate any comments on why my search for employment has reached a dead end.

A. You have made a classic error in the preparation of your resume. Your resume reads more like the history of automation than a resume. The reader must journey through 2½ pages and several generations of computers and software before reading about what you can do for them today. At the first level of screening, resumes are often scanned. Someone scanning your resume would get the impression that you might be one of the dinosaurs.

Many people screening resumes are too young to appreciate Autocoder programs or the IBM 1401, but they do understand programmer. Certainly you should list all previous positions held and provide a brief discussion of duties, but any in-depth discussions should focus on state-of-the-art skills. You have some marketable skills. Prepare a resume that draws the reader's attention to these skills.

5.4.3. **Q.** I am a mid-career, about-to-be M.B.A. Although my experience and education (M.S.) has been in food technology, I want to move out of this low growth arena into the high-tech field. I thought I could best do this through sales of computer equipment to universities, and/or to the federal government. As I read through the ads for salespeople, however, I am increasingly aware that my lack of knowledge of computerese and specific hardware/software products may prohibit me from reaching my goal.

I have been doing extensive market research and have identified several firms I believe could use my skills, but I am unsure as to how to approach them. I have a strong computer aptitude. I am building a computer and have taught myself several languages.

Any suggestions as to how I might approach these future employers?

A. Being conversant in computerese is close to the bottom of a recruiter's list of desired qualifications for a computer salesperson. Recruiters are looking for someone who can make a favorable impression and has the ability to convince customers to buy their products. As far as the technical aspects of selling hardware, you need only to demonstrate an ability and willingness to learn. Most vendors have excellent training programs.

Your qualifications are superior to the majority of applicants seeking positions in hardware sales. Approach potential employers as someone with experience, education, and interest in cross-training to the field of computers.

It would be counterproductive to mention your desire to sell to a specific market. Your initial market assignments will be based more on immediate needs than professional background.

5.4.4. **Q.** I have been a programmer for almost three years. At first I enjoyed the detail work, but now I realize that I would like to persue [sic] a computer marketing carreer [sic] and work with more global ideas.

I have no sales experience, however I do have an MBA. I havn't [sic] had much success in achieving this goal. Any advice?

A. The computer market is fiercely competitive. Vendors are seeking people with the ability to sell themselves and their product.

Consistent with this objective, vendors want people with good verbal and written communication skills. In that regard, you'll need to buy a dictionary before potential employers will take you seriously.

A misspelled word in an application raises two questions; is this the applicant's best shot? Does the applicant really care?

5.4.5.   Q. Five months ago I was the victim of a company-wide reduction in white-collar workers. After 18 years of service, primarily in programming, systems, and more recently in staff capacities, I am looking for a job in an area that already has 13 percent unemployment.

Periodically, a position opens up for an experienced programmer. I would be happy to take a programming position and then work up, but my age and recent experience are working against me. The two companies with which I interviewed were seeking people with "more current" programming skills.

I have eight years of programming experience and am confident that I will have no trouble catching up to speed. How can I convince these people that this is the case? My wife, who is not employed either, and the children refuse to discuss moving to another part of the country.

A. Why not demonstrate to prospective employers that you are upgrading your technical skills by taking a few college courses, perhaps in database management systems and structured programming techniques. If you are hired next week, you can retrain while on the job. But for now, I would recommend devoting time to developing marketable skills. On your next interview, stress your educational pursuits and how your systems experience will be complementary to any programming assignment.

If the choice is between employment elsewhere and unemployment where you are, I hope your family will reconsider.

5.4.6.   Q. How do I gracefully tell a prospective employer that I will do any work that is remotely related to computers? I have 23 years of experience in operations, programming, and systems, and I have been unemployed for eight months.

On my resume, I stated that I am seeking "a challenging position as a programmer/analyst leading to project management." How can I say that I would be happy with any type of computer work without sounding desperate?

A. How about this: "a challenging opportunity that will permit me to employ my computer expertise in areas where computing and information resources are not realizing their full potential."

5.4.7.   Q. After three years in my first and only DP position, I have received top performance reviews and pay raises above the industry averages. I am reasonably happy, but we have hired three entry-level people close to, and in one case, above my salary.

After putting myself on the block, I have received a very inviting offer with a 25 percent increase in salary. I talked informally with my immediate supervisor about the possibility of my leaving. Within the week my present employer matched the offer. Benefits considered, the new job has a slight economic advantage. Any input you might have to this decision would be appreciated.

A. Like thousands of others, you are an amateur playing a game with seasoned professionals. But the game is not over and you should know the rules before accepting or rejecting an offer. I find the rules created by a seller's market objectionable, but rules are rules.

It seems the most popular corporate MIS recruiting strategy is to get the most (not necessarily the best) for the least. The industry has adopted a system of barter where one seldom accepts the first or, in many cases, the second offer. An individual's potential for corporate contribution is often overlooked to accommodate the corporate recruiting strategy.

The game is not over until you are duly compensated for your worth. How you play the game is a matter of personal preference, but you must make a concerted effort to determine the value of your services. Don't expect any help.

5.5 PROFESSIONALISM AND CERTIFICATION

5.5.1. **Q.** I am again assessing my long-term career goals. Please help. After obtaining a bachelor's degree in accounting, I spent two years as an internal auditor and over four years in manufacturing environments working independently as a user analyst for EDP systems implementation projects. At the same time, I earned an associate degree in data processing. Because I felt I did not have enough technical background or experience to become a systems analyst or EDP auditor, I took a demotion to work as a COBOL programmer in a governmental agency for the next two years.

Recently I was reclassified as a systems analyst and feel that this is an excellent steppingstone, but the economy has threatened my job security. Without a CDP, CISA or an M.B.A., where do I go from here? The agency I work for has provided me with little state-of-the-art exposure, such as data base. Two years of programming experience is minimal qualifications and six months as a systems analyst is hardly worth mentioning.

Do you have some suggestions? There must be a niche for me.

A. You have been talking to the wrong people and probably working in the wrong place. The circumstances under which you work have instilled a lack of confidence in your abilities. A well-written resume will be well received, and prompt your consideration for meaningful positions as an analyst or an EDP auditor.

The CDP, CISA, and M.B.A. are three of many items that could be logged in the nice-to-have column, but at present are certainly not considered essential for success.

5.5.2.   Q. I have a degree in physics and am currently working in an on-line, data base environment as a programmer/analyst. I would like to get a bachelor's degree in computer science, but for family reasons, this is not possible.

Is it possible to cover up this deficiency by taking some examinations in the field that are recognized in the employment markets?

A. There are no examinations that you can take that will significantly impact your employability. The CDP (Certificate in Data Processing), CCP (Certificate in Computer Programming), and CISA (Certified Information Systems Auditor) certifications, all of which require examinations, are the most widely held and best known certifications, but they seldom impact on hiring decisions.

Author's note: The next Q&A addresses the CDP facet of the preceding Q&A in more depth.

5.5.3.   Q. Will the CDP (Certificate in Data Processing) ever be regarded with the comparable esteem of the CPA (Certified Public Accountant), PE (Professional Engineer), and so on?

A. As we carry out the routine of our daily assignments, we sometimes overlook the enormous responsibilities with which professionals in the computer/information fields are entrusted. We definitely need some mechanism to police incompetence and ensure system/data integrity.

In its current multiple-choice, machine-graded format (question content notwithstanding), I doubt that the CDP will ever be regarded with "comparable esteem." I am confident that, with a substantial overhaul, the CDP could take its place beside the CPA and others.

Other professional certification procedures are far from perfect, but they are widely recognized in the business community. Certification for the law, engineering, and accounting professions is simply more rigorous. Each requires that substantial education and experience prerequisites be met, examinations be written, and that professional peers evaluate the exams. These elements are missing in the CDP.

If the CDP format is revised to be consistent with other professional certification procedures, it may someday be regarded as comparable. If it does not, it is inevitable that one with the necessary elements will evolve.

Author's note: Apparently a DP manager shares some of my concern about the content of the CDP exam. Read on.

5.5.4.   Q. After 16 years in DP management and an M.S. in telecommunications, I considered taking the exam for a Certificate in Data Processing (CDP). To see what I might expect, I sent for a CDP exam guide. To put it mildly, I was amazed to find what the Institute for Certification of Computer Professionals (ICCP) finds relevant for CDP testing.

Because I started out wiring IBM 407 boards, I am more than familiar with ancient history. In some cases, particularly what they categorize as telecommunications, their right answer is only true in an IBM sense. In a general sense, they are often wrong.

I would lay odds that a new graduate in computer science could not pass the CDP test as it is now constituted since a great deal of the material is dated and IBM oriented. As long as this situation exists, the CDP will never be taken seriously except by the IBM old-timers who delight in arcane, and now largely moot, knowledge. The CDP seems to reflect a 1970 mindset.

Is the CDP worthwhile? If so, under what conditions is the possession of the CDP beneficial?

A. The CDP exam guide to which you refer is one author's concept of what is contained in the CDP exam, not necessarily that of the ICCP (Institute for Certification of Computer Professionals). However, I would expect the author to have a good handle on exam content.

I more or less agree with your assessment of the exam. I once stated that "the CDP is a commendable effort to provide a mechanism by which an individual can show the extent of his or her knowledge and experience in data processing and information management," but "in my opinion, the CDP examination does not accurately measure one's DP/MIS knowledge."

As to its worth, you are probably better off with the CDP than without it. Until the format is changed and the work experience and educational requirements are upgraded to be consistent with other professional certifications, the CDP will continue to receive a lukewarm to neutral endorsement from the computer community. The business community in general will continue to ignore it.

Our field is in need of a truly professional certification program and I hope that the charter member societies of the ICCP will take the bull by the horns and do it. My fear is that the CDP in its present format (multiple-choice, machine graded, minimal education/experience requirements) has too much revenue potential. This revenue would be eliminated if the exam were upgraded to a peer evaluation format.

Author's note: In the next Q&A, I suggest approaches to studying for the CDP exam.

5.5.5. **Q.** I am scheduled to take the CDP (Certificate in Data Processing) examination in May. I have been in data processing for ten years: six years as a programmer/analyst and four years with our standards group. My undergraduate degree is in business management; however, what I know about DP I have learned since starting to work (mostly through OJT). How do I prepare to take the CDP examination?

A. In my opinion, the CDP examination does not accurately measure one's DP/MIS knowledge. The exam categories do not necessarily reflect those skill areas required of the DP professional. The multiple-choice format results in an oversimplification of many of the questions; therefore, anyone taking the exam must make certain assumptions about the environment. For example, a number of questions in the management section had several correct answers depending upon what assumptions were made. Since only one answer is counted as correct, guesswork comes into play. The CDP examination needs a complete overhaul in content, format, and orientation. Because of these exam shortcomings, the manner in which you prepare for the exam may determine whether you pass or fail.

There are two basic approaches to preparing for the examination. You can either study diligently for the examination in hopes of passing all sections on the first try, or take the examination "semi-cold."

If you select the semi-cold approach, you would spend a few evenings just prior to the examination skimming over related textbooks or, perhaps CDP review manuals. The strategy to the semi-cold approach is to rely primarily on your experience and formal DP education to get you past as many of the exam sections as possible on the first try. Chances are that an experienced DPer will pass at least two parts (and possibly all five parts on the first try). Next year, your study could be concentrated on the sections that you did not pass. A word to the wise: Immediately after the examination, get together with several others who took the exam and identify those sections which you feel you may not have passed. Then, as a group, make note of the types of questions and topic areas which were emphasized. These notes will prove invaluable for next year's preparation (if needed).

The other approach requires that special attention and study be given to each of the five sections of the examination. In the long run, this approach will result in a greater knowledge and understanding of the exam material, but at the expense of as much as two or three times the effort required for the semi-cold approach.

Certainly the semi-cold approach is geared to obtaining the CDP with the least amount of effort. The obvious disadvantage is the possibility of an added year in the process. Of course this possibility also exists, to a lesser extent, with the other approach.

Periodically I receive notice of a locally sponsored CDP review seminar. Make an inquiry to your local Data Processing Management Association chapter. If no such seminar exists, set aside three or four hours a week for a review with five to ten other DPers who plan to take the exam. Chances are the cross-section of skills represented will cover all sections of the exam.

5.5.6.   Q. Last year I graduated from college and joined my father's business, presumably to sell appliances. I convinced him to buy a computer and have since automated all the company's accounting and inventory systems.

I now spend almost all my time programming or operating the systems. I enjoy my work and would like to be able to discuss it with others, but I am a one-man show.

ACM and DPMA chapters are located near by. I would like to join one so that I can talk with people of similar interests. Which one do you think would be best for a person in my position?

A. The decision to join one or the other should be based on whether or not you like the people, and the quality and orientation of the chapter activities. Chapters of the same society vary considerably from one city to the next.

I would suggest that you visit each several times. Pay particular attention to the makeup of the active membership.

One group sometimes becomes the dominant force and ultimately determines the type of programs scheduled and the topics for locally sponsored seminars. The best chapters have a healthy cross section of managers, academics, programmers, analysts, hobbyists, and vendors.

I would also be remiss not to mention that there are scores of other societies for MIS professionals, such as the Association for Computing Machinery (ACM), Society for Information Management (SIM), Association for Information Systems Professionals (AISP), and over 100 others.

5.5.7.   Q. I arrived in this country from England in 1979 as a contract programmer based out of London. I enjoyed America so much I decided to stay. At that time, I was contracted out to a company that was more than willing to hire me as a full-time senior programmer/analyst.

I then attempted to get a green card to enable me to work for an American company indefinitely. However, in about a month, I will become an illegal alien because of the annual limit on green cards. As with many things of this nature, people in certain classifications receive preference. Since I do not have an academic degree in the American sense, I do not qualify for "third preference" which would have given me a green card almost immediately. For any other preference level, it would take at least eight months to get a card and by that time I will be an illegal alien.

Another way of qualifying for third preference is to work in a career that is considered a profession. That is where you come in.

If anybody can confirm that members of the DP profession, in particular systems programmers, are indeed considered professionals, you can. I need to be able to prove to the Immigration Department that I am a professional.

A. The term *professional* is used very loosely today and is applied to everyone from dishwashers to engineers. There is no sacred list that christens those in certain disciplines as professionals. A professional has a marketable knowledge that usually takes years of study to acquire. The ancient and learned professions of law and medicine are considered professions, but not all attorneys and physicians are professionals. Professionals are committed to upholding the highest standards of their profession and to performing services to the best of their abilities.

Systems programming is not an ancient and learned profession, but it *is* a modern and learned profession. If the Immigration Department does not recognize qualified computer specialists as professionals, especially systems programmers, then they are blind to what is happening in the world today. If you meet the standards of your profession, then you are a professional.

5.5.8. Q. After presenting myself as a consultant in software engineering, one of our clients informed me that it is unlawful to do consulting in software engineering, or any other engineering, without being a registered professional engineer.

Is he correct?

A. The laws and procedures for licensing of professional engineers vary from state to state. However, the essence of each law disallows anyone from presenting themselves, either verbally or in printed material, as an engineer of any kind without being licensed as a registered professional engineer. According to the letter of the law, you cannot call yourself a software engineer and do consulting unless you have the P.E. (professional engineer) behind your name.

Not unlike other bureaucratic systems, there is a catch. To my knowledge, no state offers an examination in the area of software engineering; therefore, in order to become registered, you must take the exam in one of the more traditional areas such as electrical engineering, mechanical engineering, chemical engineering, civil engineering, industrial engineering, and so forth. If you sit for and pass the P.E. exam in any area, you can do consulting as a software engineer.

Before you panic and send for a new set of business cards, let me put this into perspective. I have known scores of vendor representatives who had "Systems Engineer" emblazoned on their business cards. Not one of them has spent one day in the pokey for this flagrant unlawful act.

5.5.9.   Q. About two months ago, I read an article that discussed the possibility of computer programmers and analysts having to pass a test and receive a license before they enter the job market.

I am presently a student in data processing and am interested in working as a programmer. Please let me know if licensing is now a requirement or if it will be soon.

A. Licensing and certification have been hot issues in the computer community during the last decade. As the public and corporate executives recognize the enormous responsibilities that programmers have over not only money but the way people live, the issue of licensing will become more intense. But for now, there is no requirement for computer programmers to be licensed, nor do I expect such a requirement in the foreseeable future.

5.5.10.   Q. I am presently employed as a computer consultant. While on one of my accounts, I came in contact with a man who was certified in computer audits. I am interested in finding out what it takes to be certified and how one goes about becoming certified. I have tried our local colleges and no one seems to know anything about it.

A. The EDP Auditor's Foundation, Inc. administers the Certified Information Systems Auditor (CISA) examination. Each year the examination is offered in approximately 20 U.S. cities and four international cities.

The content of the six-hour examination is taken from the following job areas: application systems control review; data integrity review; system development life cycle review; application development review; general operational procedures control review; security review; systems software review; maintenance review; acquisition review; data processing resource management review; and information systems audit management.

5.6 ENTREPRENEURIAL INNOVATION

5.6.1.   Q. I am a senior systems analyst with over 16 years in data processing. Over the years, I have designed and implemented several systems for the minis.
Can you tell me the best method to market these systems?

A. I cannot conceive of a more risky entrepreneurial venture than an individual entering the market for proprietary software aimed at well-established hardware. If your planned-product orientation is along the lines of standard systems, I am reluctant to offer much encouragement.

However, if you have a unique product that is state of the art and noticeably superior to existing alternatives, then opportunity does exist.

Unless you have plenty of seed money and finely tuned marketing skills, I would recommend that you first try to sell your products to an established hardware or software vendor. They will have the distribution network and sales force needed to successfully market your product.

You will increase the probability of success if you design a product that uses the full potential of recently introduced hardware. It is unlikely that you could, at this late date, grab a foothold in the portfolio of well-established proprietary software products designed specifically for the systems that you mention.

5.6.2.   Q. I have been in the data processing industry for almost 13 years. In that period I have authored and copyrighted several applications systems and have sold them locally. These systems include payroll, accounts payable, general ledger, scheduling, and others.

I would like to advertise my packages and address a much larger area. My problem is I do not know how to get started or whom to contact. My packages will run on all equipment supporting RPG II. Could you tell me what steps I would take to market my software packages?

A. Traditionally, software vendors and entrepreneurs have relied on trade publications, direct mail, direct sales, and trade shows to reach their audience. During the last few years, traveling product seminars and television have also become integral to software marketing strategy. Vendors are continually manipulating the allocation of their marketing dollars to achieve the most effective strategy. They also take advantage of "free" advertising by sending speakers to conferences and providing product releases to trade periodicals.

I don't want to discourage you, as there are many millionaires-to-be out there; however, they will make their fortunes on products that are unique or are a substantial improvement over established state-of-the-art products.

You may be able to compete locally through personal contacts, but to compete nationally with standard systems, a totally integrated data base environment is a prerequisite. Even if you have the product, you have to be a little lucky to achieve market acceptance.

The expense involved in the development, marketing, sales, and ongoing support of even the most basic product aimed at a national audience can be overwhelming. Unless you are independently wealthy or are willing to mortgage your home (and everything else), you might investigate the possibility of joining forces with a vendor that has an established distribution and support network.

For a modest investment of $2,000 to $5,000, you can test the water by leasing a booth at a regional trade show and placing small ads in a few trade publications. Be forewarned: Unless your product is aimed at an untapped audience or has some very seductive features, the response may be less than enthusiastic.

5.6.3.   Q. I will graduate this year with a degree in computer information systems and I already have two job offers, both as a business systems programmer. My parents want me to take one of these jobs, but a friend and I want to try to make it on our own.

We would like to set up our own consulting company that specializes in microcomputers. Our current part-time employer has said that he could use us both from 10 to 20 hours per week for an indefinite period (probably as long as we want to stay). However, he is not willing to pay much more than we are getting now ($7 per hour). We plan to live on what we make from him while looking for other more lucrative jobs.

Is there a demand for consultants who specialize in micros? Can a couple of 21-year-olds make a go of it in consulting?

A. The first question is easy to answer. Yes, there is a demand for such services. The second question involves too many variables for me to come up with a definitive response. Your ambition, entrepreneurial nature, technical capabilities, and the competition in the local area have an impact on whether or not you will succeed.

You have two things working against you, your age and the competition. Your abilities notwithstanding, clients are conditioned to expect consultants who exhibit the appearance of having been in the trenches for a few years. A growing cottage industry, made up primarily of former MIS professionals, is your biggest competition. Even with these obstacles, if you can exude a maturity beyond your years and you have the drive, you have a fighting chance.

Index